Onions, Leeks, & Garlic

Number Nineteen:
The W. L. Moody, Jr., Natural History Series

Onions, Leeks, & Garlic

A Handbook for Gardeners

MARIAN COONSE

TEXAS A&M UNIVERSITY PRESS
College Station

Library of Congress Cataloging-in-Publication Data

Coonse, Marian, 1912–
    Onions, leeks, and garlic : a handbook for gardeners / Marian Coonse.
— 1st ed.
        p.   cm. — (The W. L. Moody, Jr., natural history series ; no. 19)
    Includes bibliographical references (p.   ) and index.
    ISBN 0-89096-675-3 (cloth). — ISBN 0-89096-676-1 (pbk.)
    1. Onions.   2. Leeks.   3. Garlic.   I. Title.   II. Series.
SB341.C64 1995
636'.26—dc20   95-16659
                                                                    CIP

Contents

Illustrations

Tables

Preface

During the years our family owned and operated the Yankee Peddler Herb Farm, a month seldom went by that I didn't promise myself and my coworkers that I would write a book about onions. In fact, a month seldom went by that we didn't receive a number of letters loaded with questions about the complex *Allium* family.

There seemed to be more confusion about the various species of onions and garlics than about any other plant we grew. And this confusion covered just about every aspect of onion growing—how the species differed, how and when they were planted, how and when they were harvested, hardiness of the various species in the different zones, insects and diseases that might become a problem, and so on.

Because I was the bookworm in the family, it followed as a matter of course that I should be the one to search out the answers and reply to their letters. To do that intelligently required a great deal of reading *and* writing.

I'm an old hand at raising onions in Texas, so I had no problem answering questions from gardeners in the South. But ours was a mail-order business, and inquiries came from all parts of the United States, and sometimes from foreign countries as well.

Although I had lived in the North before moving to Texas and knew the climatic conditions of those regions, my years there were not spent growing onions, so I didn't have that information from firsthand experience. But I did have access to most everything of value that had been written on the subject, and volumes not already on my shelves were gradually added.

What a help it would have been to have been able to draw the needed information from a single book, rather than having to wade through numerous volumes, gleaning the answers in bits and pieces. As far as I knew, only one really comprehensive book about onions had ever been published, and it was out of print.

The more letters I received, the more books I had to open; and the more books I had to open, the more certain I was that a new book on the subject was needed. But I was too busy to write it. . . . I had an herb farm to help run.

In the meantime my library grew, my knowledge of onions grew, and my files grew fat with reference notes and carbons of letters to our customers. The fatter my files grew, the more my determination grew that the book would someday be a reality.

Then came the day when we decided to retire, and the herb farm was sold. At last I had time to write. Out of the files came the reference notes and letters, and out of the confusion in the minds of some of our customers the skeleton of this book was born.

So here it is, based on the needs of onion growers throughout the United States, from whence most of the letters came. In *Onions: A Handbook for Gardeners* I have tried to touch on all aspects of the subject, from onions' earliest days to the present.

Chapters 1 and 2 present a brief history of onions and their development through the ages, with instructions for modern-day methods of planting, growing, harvesting, drying, and storing. Chapter 3 lists and describes all the important members of the *Allium* family. Also included in this chapter is a section on the wild members of the onion tribe that are sometimes used for food. Chapter 4 deals with insects, and Chapter 5 discusses diseases that may be encountered when growing onions.

A good part of the scientific information throughout the text was supplied by the U.S. Department of Agriculture (USDA) in the form of reports given by USDA entomologists and pathologists. Other information came from universities and state agricultural experiment stations all across America. Many of the photos were also supplied by these departments.

I am most grateful to Dessert Seed Company, Inc., El Centro, California, for supplying photographs (and for not running out of patience while I got this all together).

I'm indebted to many others who helped open doors for me—
Dr. Gilbert McCollum, research geneticist, Vegetable Labora-
tory, Horticultural Science Institute, Beltsville, Maryland; W. R.
Simpson, research professor of plant pathology, University of Idaho;
C. E. Peterson, research horticulturist, University of Wisconsin;
Harold E. Moore, Jr., Liberty Hyde Bailey Professor of Botany,
Cornell University; D. E. Lousley, vice consul and assistant trade
commissioner, Canadian Consulate General's office, Dallas, Texas;
Eugene Whelan, minister of agriculture, Ottawa, Canada; and to
all U.S. seed companies, from coast to coast and from border to
border, who sent catalogs and furnished information about onion
varieties best grown in their area.

To all these kind people, to our erstwhile customers who posed
the questions in the first place, and especially to my family and
coworkers, who kept prodding me, I am profoundly grateful.

Onions, Leeks, & Garlic

I

The Culinary Jewels

ॐ

ONIONS FROM ANTIQUITY TO THE PRESENT

Legend says that when Satan stepped out of the Garden of Eden after the fall of man, onions sprang up from the spot where he placed his right foot and garlic from where his left foot touched.

Diners who are fastidiously breath conscious would gladly give the Devil his due when it comes to garlic, but few lovers of epicurean delicacies would ever believe that Satan had a hand (or a foot) in the origin of the onion.

The common onion has been regarded as a culinary jewel since time began, and is said to be fourth in line as a seasoning ingredient of meats and main dishes, topped only by butter, salt, and pepper.

"It is cherished everywhere in kitchen gardens," wrote John Gerard in *The Herbal* in 1597. Earlier records, however, show that onions were valued as food crops hundreds of years before the days of Gerard, so many years in fact that their place of origin is unknown.

According to early writers, onions and garlic have always been favorite foods in Egypt. In *Onions and Their Allies*, Henry A. Jones and Louis K. Mann tell us (p. 18) that "labourers eating onions are depicted in mastabas (tombs) of as early as the Ist and II Dynasties (about 3200–2780 B.C.)."

Herbalists and agricultural writers from Hippocrates on down—

Palladius, Pliny, Dioscorides, Columella, and others—mention onions in their writings. But the most significant record of the onion's early popularity is the Bible (Num. 11:5), during the time of the Pharaohs, when the Hebrews were fleeing to the Promised Land.

In the wilderness they hungered for the foods they had left behind and complained bitterly to Moses. "We remember the fish which we did eat in Egypt freely; the cucumbers, and the melons, and the leeks, and the onions, and the garlic."

Herodotus, born almost five hundred years before Christ, wrote that during his time there was an inscription on the Great Pyramid stating the sum expended for onions, garlic, and radishes consumed by the laborers during its construction: sixteen hundred silver talents, an amount equivalent to thirty thousand dollars to fifty thousand dollars!

Sir John Gardner Wilkinson, a distinguished geologist of the 1800s, who spent more than twelve years studying the ancient monuments of Egypt, records that onions and garlic are frequently featured in religious paintings.

In *Onions and Their Allies*—probably the most comprehensive volume ever written on the subject, Jones and Mann comment on this and other customs that prevailed in ancient Egypt:

> In Egypt the onion is mentioned as one of the funerary offerings as early as the IIIrd and IVth Dynasties, during the early part of the Pyramid age (about 2780–2100 B.C.). Onions are depicted on the banquet tables of great feasts—both large, peeled onions and slender, immature ones. They were among the offerings placed upon the altars of the gods, together with gourds, cakes, beef, goose or wild fowl, grapes, figs, wine, and the head of the victim. Frequently a priest is holding onions in his hand or covering an altar with a bundle of their leaves and roots. In ordinary offerings they were bound together in a single bundle. On the other hand, it is reported that certain priests abstained from them as unlawful food. In mummies, onions have frequently been found in the pelvic regions of the body, in the thorax, flattened against the ears, and in front of the collapsed eyes. Flowering onions have been

found on the chest, and onions have been found attached to the soles of the feet and along the legs. (p. 19)

Onions and garlic have also figured prominently as a universal remedy among the living. In early medicine, the bulbs were prepared in syrups, poultices, ointments, and lotions for treating coughs, colds, croup, wounds, and skin problems of all kinds—from boils and pimples to ulcers and scrofulous sores. Onion concoctions were an accepted remedy for hemorrhoids, rheumatism, gout, epilepsy, worms, asthma, consumption, and other lung diseases, and were used as a diuretic.

According to Gerard's *Herbal,* onions not only restored the health of those afflicted with foregoing ailments, but could also cure obesity and baldness. The juice rubbed on a bald head in the sun, he said, would even cause hair to grow.

The U.S. Dispensatory of Medicine (1877) doesn't go that far, but it does support some of Gerard's claims. It points out that the bulbs of onion and garlic contain a volatile oil consisting largely of allyl sulfide, which is effective in treating certain ailments:

> By virtue of its volatile oil the onion taken in moderate quantities is a stimulant to the stomach and promotes digestion, but in large quantities is apt to cause gastric uneasiness. It is slightly rubefacient, said to be diuretic, and belongs among those expectorants to be employed in the advanced stages of subacute *bronchitis* or in chronic *bronchitis.* Although the onion has been asserted to exercise a marked influence on nitrogenous metabolism it can scarcely be doubted that any apparent influence which it may exert in the direction spoken of is secondary to its action upon digestion.
>
> Onion poultices are somewhat effective as a counter-irritant and nerve stimulant in cases of *bronchitis* or *pneumonia* in young children, with nervous symptoms. (p. 1525)

Throughout the ages, onions and allied species—garlic, leeks, shallots, and chives—have been considered members of the lily family. With the publication of *Hortus Third* in 1975, many nomenclature changes became official in the plant world. This new standard authority now places onions in the amaryllis family.

In contrast with the tender nature of some of its newly claimed relatives—tuberose, crinum, spider lily, and others—the onion is one of the hardiest plants in the garden, and therefore one of the earliest crops to be planted in spring.

Wherever its origin, and whatever its family tree, this culinary jewel that is as old as time itself has spread to all countries where the crop can be grown at some season of the year.

There is no record of when the cultivated onion was first introduced into North America. The first printed mention concerning the New World was titled *New England's Prospect* and was published by William Wood in London in 1634. Wood, a colonist, mentioned that onions were cultivated in Massachusetts at that time. We have no way of knowing whether the colonists brought seeds of the various types with them or found them growing here.

Later publications show that more than one variety was cultivated during those early years. Six varieties of onions are mentioned in the *American Gardener's Calendar*, published by Bernard McMahon in 1806. This was the first important horticultural work to be published in the United States, and it remained a standard reference work for more than half a century.

The number of known varieties continued to increase, either by discovery of plants growing in the New World or by importation of seed from England and the Continent. *The Field and Garden Vegetables of America*, published in Boston in 1863 by Fearing Burr, Jr., lists, describes, and gives instructions for propagating fourteen varieties of onions.

In Europe, a French nurseryman named Pierre Vilmorin compiled information on onions that he knew about. In 1883 he published *Les plantes potagères*, naming sixty varieties and describing them as flat, flattened, disk-form, spherical, spherical-flattened, pear-shaped, or long. Modern nurserymen are less explicit in defining the bulb shapes of onions than was Vilmorin back in 1883. Today they are known as globe, flattened globe, high globe, spindle, Spanish, flat, thick-flat, granex, and top-shaped.

With the coming of hybridization, the number of onion varieties began to skyrocket, and has been skyrocketing ever since. It is doubtful that anyone knows how many varieties exist today, and even more doubtful that it is known how many once-popular sorts have fallen from favor in the United States since hybridization began. Consider, for instance, a few of the first-raters that were offered in Burpee's 1888 catalog: Earliest White Queen, New Golden Queen, Giant Rocca (red, yellow, and reddish brown), Silver White Etna, Pale Red Etna, Silver Ball, and Tripoli. And we mustn't overlook Burpee's New Mammoth Silver King, a spectacular giant that had been introduced by them four years earlier. This onion, they said, was second in size only to New Mammoth Pompeii—another popular choice in those days—and often attained weights up to 4¾ pounds and diameters to seven inches.

When we contemplate the size of this beauty and read that its flesh was snowy white, so sweet and tender it could be eaten raw, like an apple, we wonder what could have warranted dropping it from their list.

Was Silver King dethroned because of shortcomings that were not apparent during the early years of its reign? A susceptibility to insects and diseases, perhaps? A poor yielder? A premature bolter? Or was it discontinued simply because it was difficult to propagate? Such characteristics are important if a variety is to survive.

Equally important—to the homemaker at least—is the wide range of varieties that have survived. Today's market offers flavors for every palate and varieties for every use. Onions have been developed that are sweet and juicy for salads, strong and pungent for adding zest to cooked foods; others not only are pungent but also have a high dry-matter content, making them a better choice for drying.

Commercial dehydration of onions, which began in the United States during the Civil War, has become big business and has lightened the tasks of homemakers throughout the world. Each year, many thousands of pounds of dehydrated onions find their way to grocery shelves in the form of onion flakes, onion powder, onion salt, onion rings, onion dips; in meat products such as corned beef hash, sausages, and cold cuts; as seasonings in canned soups, dried soup mixes, tomato sauces, catsup, and other items.

Through scientific breeding methods, onion growers have been able to eliminate certain undesirable qualities while perpetuating favorable characteristics. They have given us not only onions that are outstanding in shape, size, uniformity, and time of maturity, but also varieties that are resistant to the attack of insects—notably thrips, the most destructive pest of all—and to various plant diseases, such as pink root, smut, mildew, purple blotch, and tip and leaf blight.

Plant breeders have come a long way with this culinary jewel since the time of the pharaohs.

IMPROVED VARIETIES THROUGH HYBRIDIZATION

According to Robert Cook, in *A Chronology of Genetics*, hybridization had its beginnings during the Stone Age, possibly as many as twenty-five thousand years ago, when Neolithic peoples experimented with the crossbreeding of species and varieties of cattle and dogs.

Hybridization of plants came much later, during the seventeenth century. Until then, it wasn't even known that plants had sex organs, much less that they'd respond to extramarital relations outside their own kind.

The discovery of sexual processes in plants was made by a German physician and botanist, Rudolph Jakob Camerarius, who had been observing the sexual relations of plants in the botanical garden he oversaw at Tubingen, Germany. After extensive observation and experimentation, he realized the importance of the stamen and pistil and the part played by pollen in fertilization.

His findings were published in 1694—a fifty-page letter on the sex life of plants, *De Sexu Plantarum Epistola*. This letter was to become famous because it put on record convincing evidence that plants are sexual organisms.

This was followed by Thomas Fairchild's production of the first artificial plant hybrid in England in about 1717.

On the heels of Camerarius' discovery and Fairchild's success, seed-breeding establishments began cropping up all over, the most notable of which was Vilmorin-Andrieux et Cie of France (1727).

"In the next 50 years," Cook says, "there was a veritable wave of hybridization."

Josef G. Koelreuter, a German botanist, was another pioneer in the investigation of hybridization in plants. He conducted numerous experiments, and his findings, which included 136 successful results in hybridization, were published between 1761 and 1766. His reports definitely established plant hybridization as a scientific pursuit and were studied with great interest by those who followed—Dean Herbert of Manchester, Von Mons, Gaertner, and others.

It was Gregor Johann Mendel, however, whom history credits with being the founder of plant breeding, even though his experiments did not come until the 1850s, a hundred years after those of Koelreuter.

Mendel was an Austrian monk of the monastary at Brünn, and it was there in the cloister gardens that he conducted his investigations on plant hybrids. The subject of his experiments was peas, but the theory he proposed has been shown to hold with other plants, and with all living creatures as well. His theory was based on heredity.

Experiments made before Mendel's time had shown only the forms hybrids took when different species or varieties were crossed. Mendel, however, considered this only the first step. What about the offspring of the hybrid? What form or forms would it take?

Mendel's *Book of Popular Science* offers an excellent report on his views:

> Among all the experiments made, not one has been carried out to such an extent and in such a way as to make it possible to determine the number of different forms under which the offspring of hybrids appear, or to arrange these forms with certainty according to their separate generations, or definitely ascertain their statistical relations.

For eight years Mendel experimented with plants in the monastery gardens—crossing, backcrossing, observing, making notes.

He learned that certain inherited qualities are strong and others are weak—or, in his own words, "dominant" and "recessive."

When tall peas were crossed with dwarf peas, for instance, the tall character dominated and all the F_1 hybrids were tall. The recessive (dwarf) character had entirely disappeared from the first generation. But it reappeared in the next. Only three out of every four plants of this second generation—the F_2 hybrids—were tall; the fourth one was dwarf.

By self-fertilizing the tall plants of the F_2 hybrids, he produced a third generation in which *all* the plants were tall. The same held true in breeding F_2 dwarfs.

Then he bred from a third generation, and he found that the dwarfs remained dwarf in their offspring, not only in this generation but in the generations that followed. The tall characteristic had been bred out of them.

But what about the three-fourths of the F_2 generation that was tall? They all possessed the dominant characteristic of their parents, the F_1 hybrids, and of one of their grandparents, the tall variety of pea. Would the recessive characteristic of the other grandparent, the dwarf pea, reappear in the third generation?

It did. In breeding from the tall plants of this second generation, Mendel found that they were not all alike in their genetic constitution. Only one-third of this F_3 generation was tall; the other two-thirds had inherited the dwarf genes of their dwarf grandparents.

With the fourth generation came success. When he self-fertilized the talls of the third generation, all of their offspring were tall, and those plants—as well as all plants of the generations that followed—were tall.

As for the remaining two-thirds of the third generation, the plants that had inherited their parents' and grandparents' genes, they were just like their parents, and their offspring came out again in the ratio of three talls to one dwarf, as before.

Mendel had found what he was searching for—proof that, through selective breeding, based on hereditary factors, a pure strain could be hybridized.

Although the same principles applied to all plants, the hybrid-

Dr. Henry A. Jones, "Father of the hybrid onion," inspects self-pollination facilities at Dessert Seed Company onion breeding grounds at El Centro, California. To avoid contamination by foreign pollen, the flower heads are enclosed in metal screen cages, and flies are put in the cages to pollinate the plants. At the base of each cage is a detachable cloth sleeve, which is tied tightly around the flower stems below the cage, to prevent the flies' escape. Courtesy Dessert Seed Co.

ization of onions was not commercially feasible until 1940, more than a century after Mendel had pointed the way.

H. A. Jones and A. E. Clarke explain why in *The Story of Hybrid Onions:*

> In the ordinary onion, male and female parts are in the same flower (the perfect flower), and thus each plant is capable of pollinating itself. To get hybrid seed it is therefore necessary to remove the pollen-containing anthers of the female parent, a procedure known as emasculation. Emasculation is not so easily performed with the onion as with corn, whose male and female parts are entirely separate. In corn, emasculation consists merely in re-

moving the tassel. In the onion, the male and female parts are close together, and emasculation is tedious and difficult, because the pollen-bearing anthers must be carefully snipped out with tweezers—a process entirely too expensive for commercial production.

This obstacle, however, was surmounted when Jones found a male-sterile (female) plant in the onion-breeding plots of the University of California at Davis in 1925. This plant, whose flowers were not perfect and therefore contained no fertile pollen, was destined to be the forerunner of practically all hybrid onion seed. For breeding purposes, it was given the pedigree number 13-53.

But all was not yet clear sailing, because the plant Jones found was the only one of its kind in the field. It had five flower stems, but instead of seeds, the flower heads were packed with small sets, or bulbils—136 in all. Before the plant could be of commercial value its number would have to be increased.

From 1925 on, the variety known as 13-53 was propagated vegetatively by planting the small flower head sets, each of which would develop into a large bulb by the end of the season and produce more flower head sets at maturity.

In time, it was possible to begin tests. Crosses were made between the female line 13-53 and other red varieties. Some of the results were outstanding. For example, California Hybrid Red No. 1, which was introduced in 1944, was a cross between a rather small, thick-flat, early-maturing onion named Lord Howe Island and Jones' pedigree number 13-53, a large, spindle-shaped, slow-bolting beauty commonly known as Italian Red.

The offspring of this union was globe-shaped—large like the mother, roundish like the father, and handsomer and heavier than either parent. The hybrids inherited the best characteristics of each: the early maturity of the male parent, Lord Howe Island, and the delayed bolting habit of the female line, Italian Red.

To continue a newly developed strain, it is necessary to perpetuate the female line, and this is done by continuously backcrossing to the same male parent. With each backcrossing the female plants look more and more like the male parent, and after four or five generations there is no difference in appearance. From then on, the progeny from seed comes true to the parents. But, as Mendel proved, seeds saved from first generations of a hybrid revert to the parent varieties, or may not be fertile at all.

Confusing? You bet! And since most of us don't know a boy onion from a girl onion, it would seem that the matrimonial affairs of this ever-growing family are better left to the plant scientists, who know what they're doing.

With the many varieties, shapes, and sizes of onions offered on the market today, who needs to play Cupid in the onion patch anyhow?

PLAN AHEAD FOR A BOUNTIFUL HARVEST

Any type of soil—sandy loam, silty loam, clay loam, alluvial—will grow onions, but it must be abundantly fertile, well drained, and well prepared. It should be loose and friable, to allow for proper expansion of the bulbs, and have at least a moderate amount of organic matter to help hold moisture and improve aeration and fertility. Nitrogen, phosphorus, and potash are required in relatively large amounts to produce a bountiful harvest. Unless these needs are met, the onion crop is almost certainly doomed to failure.

Sandy loam, for example, is usually deficient in fertility and has little moisture-holding capacity. Clay and alluvial soils are generally fertile, but difficult to work because the fine, sticky particles tend to run together and turn hard as cement after a heavy rain.

Turning under a green manure crop a few weeks before planting is an excellent way to correct these problems. Alfalfa, vetch, buckwheat, oats, rye, clover, peas, beans, mustard, kale, and weeds are just a few crops that can add humus to the soil.

This is not a new idea. According to USDA agronomists A. J. Pieters and Roland McKee in *The Use of Cover and Green-Manure Crops*, the Greeks were using this method of soil improvement three hundred years before Christ, and the planting of lupines and beans for soil improvement was a common practice in the early years of the Roman Empire. The Chinese wrote about the fertilizing value of grass and weeds hundreds of years before our era. The American colonists continued the practice, planting and turning under as green manure such crops as buckwheat, oats, and rye, all of which added humus, and the partridge pea and other members of the legume family to add both organic matter and nitrogen to the soil. Gardeners who realize the value of green manure crops are still improving their soils with this method today.

Nature doesn't allow fertile land to lie barren, nor should we. This is particularly true in the South, where something can be growing every month of the year. Instead of keeping the garden "tilled clean" between seasons, why not plant a cover crop— broadcast a few handfuls of seed, and feed the land by tilling the young plants under when garden time approaches again.

"Nothing is more vital to good soil management than providing for the regular and systematic return of organic matter to the soil." So stated Gove Hambridge, principal research writer, USDA Office of Information, forty years ago in the *USDA Yearbook* for 1938 (p. 22). This statement is even truer now than it was then, because in recent years many gardeners have been relying more and more on chemical fertilizers, not realizing that these chemicals feed only the plant—not the soil.

In the top six inches of our gardens are billions of microorganisms. They cannot live without organic matter to feed on, and without these microorganisms the soil itself becomes lifeless. *No amount of chemical plant food will generate productivity in dead, decomposed rock particles.* And that is all that soil is without organic matter.

USDA experiments have shown that onions do not do well in soils that are very acid; pH 6 to 8 is best. USDA literature also reminds us that onions are shallow-rooted and need constant surface moisture to nourish these roots. With moisture, new roots continue to form throughout most of the growing season; without it, these new roots cannot form, and growth is checked. When this happens, even for a short period, the outer scales begin to mature. Then, when moisture is again available, the inner scales resume growth and the resulting harvest may consist of bulbs that are split or double.

Research has shown that even more moisture is needed from the time the plants start bulbing until they start maturing. When maturing begins, the soil should be allowed to dry out as much as possible, but until then the moisture level must be maintained to produce a bountiful harvest. This can best be done by growing the crop in soil that is rich in humus (well-decomposed organic matter).

Humus-rich soil is dark and has a spongy texture that not only retains moisture but also allows excess water to drain away. More important, humus is the main indirect source of food for plants.

Peat moss, barnyard manure, as well as worm castings and excrement from other soil-inhabiting organisms, add humus to the soil. Carcasses of insects, worms, animals, even the micro-organisms that feed on the decaying remains, are regarded as organic matter. In time these organisms too will die, decay, and become humus. It is decayed plant material, usually crop residues—dead roots, leaves, fruits, and stems of plants—that is the source for most of the soil's humus.

Where space is available, alternate sections of the garden can be set aside each year for planting the green manure crop—broadcasting it by hand, then raking it lightly to cover. Soon young shoots will be poking through the earth, and the area will become a solid blanket of green. Spring-planted green manure crops are usually tilled under in the fall; fall-planted crops are tilled under in spring.

If space is limited, the green manure crop can be planted between the rows. Or, if yours is a postage-stamp garden and too small for row planting, you can at least bury your kitchen garbage, between the plants if necessary.

During the years we operated Yankee Peddler Herb Farm, where we grew vegetables as well as herbs, we spaced our rows not less than three feet apart. With the furrower attachment on our tiller, we opened a trench down the center between two rows. In this trench our kitchen scraps were buried—potato peelings, vegetable trimmings, eggshells, coffee grounds, paper napkins; anything that came out of the earth could go back in.

A shovel stood sentinel duty, marking the area where the last material was buried and ready to cover with soil the next batch from the kitchen. When this row was completely filled in, another furrow was made between two other rows, and the process started all over again. By the time planting time rolled around again, this organic material in the trenches had decayed, enriching the soil, and it was in this area that the new crops were planted.

We were also fortunate in having a lot of clippings and residue from the greenhouses to increase the humus content of our soil, because when you grow potted herbs for sale, pruning and clipping is a never-ending job.

During summer, when the Texas sun beat down on our gardens like white heat from a blast furnace, these clippings were used as mulch. They conserved moisture around the plants, and the aromatic fragrance of the herbs served as insect repellent for other plants in the garden. Following the harvest, the mulch was tilled into the soil.

With this method, all becomes humus within a few weeks, improving the soil's tilth and moisture-holding capacity and increasing the population of our underground "plowmen," the earthworms.

But most important of all, this regular and systematic return of organic matter to the soil will keep the billions of microorganisms in our soil alive, and they in turn will keep our plants alive.

If our soil is to feed us, we first must feed our soil!

2

Guide to Growing Onions

❧

CHOOSING THE RIGHT VARIETY FOR YOUR CLIMATE

Among the onion varieties grown in the United States, there are many types that differ in bulb size, shape, and color. Some are more pungent in flavor than others; some are better keepers.

As gardeners, we need to know the time to maturity of the various types; how tolerant they are to disease, insects, sunscald, high and low temperatures; and, most important, whether the variety we're selecting will do well in our area, or if it is adapted to a region far to our north or south.

We are courting failure if we choose our onions simply by color—whether they are red, yellow, brown, or white.

No one onion is suited to all areas. A variety that will do well in the North may be a total failure in the South, and vice versa, for most varieties are limited in adaptation from one extreme region to another.

You would think that when an onion plant has been growing a certain number of weeks, it would be time for it to mature. But the age of the plant is not the deciding factor. Bulb formation is influenced by the length of the day (the number of daylight hours in a twenty-four-hour period), and this day length is not the same for all varieties.

Equally important is the temperature at the time the correct day length for bulb formation is reached. If average daily temperatures are under 60° F., bulbs will not form, regardless of the number of daylight hours.

When the minimum temperature *and* the right day length are reached—whichever the variety—bulbing begins. From then on the onions develop very rapidly. It is this point that determines the adaptability of a variety to an area.

For example, Bermuda, Creole, Early Grano, and some of the hybrids that do well in the South mature when days are short. These extra-early varieties, which begin bulbing when days are only twelve hours long, are not recommended for direct seeding in the North. By April or May, the time when onions are usually planted in the North, days are getting longer and have already passed the minimum for bulbing. Seed started this late will produce plants with only a few leaves and a small bulb. To grow large bulbs of these varieties in the North, plants are usually started in a greenhouse or hotbed, or shipped in from the South.

By the same token, late-maturing (long-day) varieties—for example, Ebenezer, Wethersfield, Globe types—that give a good yield in the North are almost impossible as a spring crop in the South. Temperatures in the South have already begun to soar by the time the thirteen to fourteen hours of daylight required for bulb development of these varieties is reached, and plants suffer from sunscald, thrips, and pink root. Sweet Spanish comes closest to being successful in both regions, because it is somewhat resistant to these problems.

When late-maturing varieties are planted in the South, the tops dry up prematurely and, again, the result is only a very small bulb.

Unfortunately, most retail seed catalogs offer the gardener very little help in making the right selection for a specific region. And, in the few catalogs in which such advice is given, it is usually buried in the fine print and often overlooked. As a result, gardeners in all regions are swayed by mouth-watering illustrations and fanciful phrases—firm, crisp, tasty, uniform, high yielder, good keeper.

How much more profitable it would be, both for the gardener and the seedsman (through repeat sales) if short-day and long-day onions were designated as such. What's wrong with saying: "These

Granex onions grown in the Southwest—Texas, New Mexico, Arizona, and California—are shipped by truck and rail to markets in the northern United States and Canada. Courtesy Dessert Seed Co.

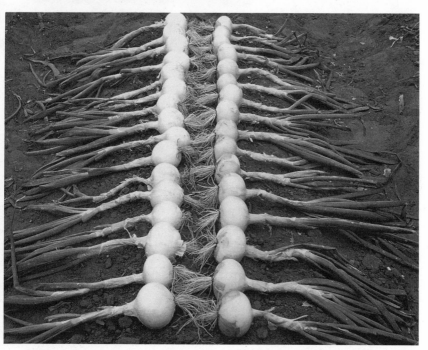

Dessex is a short-day hybrid that can hold its own in field-day inspections or in the kitchen. The bright yellow scales adhere well during harvesting and handling, and the slightly pungent flesh stays firm and crisp up to four or five months if stored under dry, well-ventilated conditions. Courtesy Dessert Seed Co.

Texas Early Grano 502 PRR is proudly displayed during field-day inspection. This standard variety was released by the Texas Agricultural Experiment Station in 1944. Courtesy Dessert Seed Co.

Amigo is a favorite sweet Spanish onion that produces large, globe-shaped bulbs with fairly heavy scales that adhere well during handling and storage. Transplants grown in the South are shipped to northern gardeners for spring planting. Courtesy Dessert Seed Co.

San Joaquin—named for the San Joaquin Valley of California, to which it is especially adapted—is a good choice for those who like onions firm, crisp, and exceptionally mild. This standard variety, released by the California Agricultural Experiment Station and the U.S. Department of Agriculture in 1941, remains popular. Courtesy Dessert Seed Co.

Fiesta is a Spanish-type hybrid that can be used where other late-maturing Spanish varieties are not well adapted. It combines high yield with the long-keeping qualities of the better hybrid cooking onions. Courtesy Dessert Seed Co.

Red Grano, a standard culinary jewel for southern gardens, has attractive, dark red outer scales, and the red color usually extends to the center of the bulb. Its mild flavor makes it a favorite in salads. Courtesy Dessert Seed Co.

Bullring is a newer Spanish-type hybrid that produces large, golden-bronze bulbs with hard, pungent flesh. It is a good onion for mechanical harvesting and long storage. Courtesy Dessert Seed Co.

are the best varieties for growing in the North" or "These are the varieties recommended for growing in the South"? Without such guidance how are you, the gardener, going to find which varieties will produce best in your climate?

One way is to buy your onion seed from a dealer in your area. Your local feed and seed store is a good source. Bulk seeds are cheaper than buying by the packet, and these merchants stock only varieties that are adapted to their region.

If you must buy by mail, make your selection from a seed company located in your general area of the country. If their test gardens and seed-producing areas are in the same general latitude as your garden, chances are the varieties they offer will do well for you.

Also to be considered is the fact that seed companies purchase seeds grown in other parts of the country for resale to their mail-order customers in those areas. This is especially true with companies that publish catalogs for national distribution. There are seed companies that publish regional catalogs, however, with special emphasis on varieties that are suitable for their particular climate.

The best way to be sure of which onions will produce in your climate is to call your local county agent. He or she will be happy to answer your questions, or will mail the information you need. Better yet, stop by the office. You'll be amazed at the informative material the agent can supply: gardening bulletins, circulars, fact sheets, and newsletters, all written by experts and focused on growing conditions in your specific area. Most of these are free, although there is a nominal charge for a few of the more elaborate booklets.

Another bureau offering valuable gardening information is the Cooperative Extension Service. This is a publicly supported organization of the U.S. Department of Agriculture and the land grant university (state college) system.

Each state has at least one agriculture experiment station (see Appendix). At these stations research goes on year after year, crossing and backcrossing various strains of onions in an effort to breed out undesirable characteristics, and to breed in the best.

Table 1. Short-day Onion Varieties

STANDARD VARIETIES

Variety	Days	Size	Color	Shape	Flavor	Storage
Texas Grano 1015Y	180	Very large	Yellow	Flat globe	Very mild	Medium
Texas Grano 1025Y	185	Very large	Yellow	Round	Mild	Medium
Texas Grano 1030Y	190	Large	Yellow	Round	Slightly pungent	Medium
Texas Grano 1105Y	190	Large	Yellow	Round	Slightly pungent	Medium
Texas Grano 438	190	Very large	Yellow	Flat globe	Slightly pungent	Medium
Dorado	190	Medium	Yellow	Round	Pungent	Medium
Perla	190	Medium	White	Round	Pungent	Medium
California Early Red	194	Thick flat	Red	Medium	Pungent	Short
Regal	188	Large	Red	Flat globe	Slightly pungent	Short
Colossal	181	Very large	Yellow	Flat globe	Slightly pungent	Short
Nu-Mex BR-1	185	Medium	Yellow	Flat globe	Mild	Medium
Ringer	179	Large	Yellow	Top shape	Mild	Short
Contessa	165	Medium	White	Globe	Mild	Short

HYBRIDS

Variety	Days	Size	Color	Shape	Flavor	Storage
Primavera	160	Medium-large	Yellow	Shallow top	Mild	Short
Savannah Sweet	160	Medium-large	Yellow	Thick, flat	Mild	Short
Rojo	185	Large	Red	Flat globe	Slightly pungent	Medium
Brilliant	180	Medium	White	Globe	Slightly pungent	Short
Tampico	185	Large	White	Globe	Slightly pungent	Short
Early Premium	165	Medium	Yellow	Flat globe	Slightly pungent	Medium-long
Gold Rush	168	Medium	Yellow	Flat globe	Slightly pungent	Medium
Gran Prix	168	Large	Yellow	Flat globe	Slightly pungent	Medium
Special 38	176	Large	Yellow	Flat globe	Slightly pungent	Medium

Table 2. Medium-day Onion Varieties

STANDARD VARIETIES

Variety	Days	Size	Color	Shape	Flavor	Storage
Italian Red Torpedo	220	Large	Red	Torpedo	Slightly pungent	Very short
New Mexico White Grano	195	Large	White	Top shape	Slightly pungent	Short
Paradise	200	Large	White	Globe	Slightly pungent	Medium
Ben Shemen	210	Large	White	Globe	Slightly pungent	Medium
New Mexico Yellow Grano	195	Large	Yellow	Top shape	Slightly pungent	Short
Texspan	205	Medium-large	Brown	Globe	Slightly pungent	Medium-long

HYBRIDS

Variety	Days	Size	Color	Shape	Flavor	Storage
Mid Star	100/225	Very large	White	Globe	Slightly pungent	Short
Cimarron	92/218	Large	Yellow	Globe	Slightly pungent	Short-medium
Candy	160	Jumbo	White	Flat globe	Slightly pungent	Short
Armada	122	Large	Yellow	Flat globe	Slightly pungent	Short
Cache	114	Large	Yellow	Globe	Slightly pungent	Short
Fiesta	110	Medium	Yellow	Globe	Slightly pungent	Short
Maya	110	Medium	Yellow	Globe	Slightly pungent	Short
Vega	117	Large	Yellow	Globe	Slightly pungent	Short
Yule	113	Large	Yellow	Tapered globe	Slightly pungent	Short

Table 3. Long-day Onion Varieties

STANDARD VARIETIES

Variety	Days	Size	Color	Shape	Flavor	Storage
Bennies Red	108	Large	Red	Top globe	Pungent	Short
Blanco Duro	120	Large	White	Blocky globe	Pungent	Medium-long
New York Early	94	Large	Yellow	Globe	Pungent	Short
White Ebenezer	110	Medium	White	Flat	Pungent	Medium
Y.S.S. Valencia	130	Large	Yellow	Globe	Pungent	Short

HYBRIDS-NORTH

Variety	Days	Size	Color	Shape	Flavor	Storage
Carmen Red	118	Large	Red	Blocky globe	Pungent	Medium-long
Tango	112	Large	Red	Globe	Pungent	Medium-long
Capable	102	Large	Yellow	High globe	Pungent	Long
Cuprum	112	Large	Brown	High globe	Pungent	Very long
EYG No. 155	96	Medium-large	Yellow	Globe	Pungent	Medium
Paragon	106	Large	Brown	Blocky globe	Pungent	Very long
Benchmark	110	Medium	Brown	Globe	Pungent	Very long
Blitz	100	Medium	Brown	Globe	Pungent	Very long
Citadel	105	Medium	Brown	Globe	Pungent	Very long
Crusader	125	Large	Brown	Tall globe	Pungent	Very long
Flame	110	Medium	Brown	Globe	Pungent	Very long
Fortress	110	Medium	Brown	Globe	Pungent	Very long
Garrison	115	Medium	Brown	Globe	Pungent	Very long
Spartan Banner 80	120	Large	Brown	Tall globe	Pungent	Very long
Sweet Sandwich	115	Large	Brown	Globe	Pungent	Very long
Taurus	105	Medium	Brown	Globe	Pungent	Very long
Summit	106	Large-jumbo	Brown	Globe	Pungent	Long
Zenith	110	Large-jumbo	Brown	Globe	Pungent	Long
Apex	110	Large-jumbo	Brown	Globe	Pungent	Long
Fuego	108	Large	Red	Globe	Pungent	Medium
Sterling	115	Large-jumbo	White	Globe	Pungent	Short
First Edition	110	Medium	Brown	Globe	Pungent	Long

Table 3. Long-day Onion Varieties, continued
HYBRIDS-NORTH

Variety	Days	Size	Color	Shape	Flavor	Storage
Avalanche	128	Large	White	Globe	Pungent	Short
Brahma	110	Medium-large	Brown	Blocky globe	Pungent	Long
Bravado	122	Large	White	Globe	Pungent	Short
Cima	116	Large	Yellow	Globe	Pungent	Long
Golden Cascade	105	Large	Yellow	Globe	Pungent	Medium-long
Magnum	108	Large	Yellow	High globe	Pungent	Medium-long
Merit	120	Very large	Yellow	Globe	Pungent	Short
Valdez	128	Very large	Yellow	Globe	Pungent	Medium
Valiant	114	Large	Brown	Blocky globe	Pungent	Long
Winner	116	Large	Brown	Globe	Pungent	Long

Scientists are busy in a never-ending quest to develop varieties with greater uniformity of shape, color, time to maturity, edibleness, and vigor, as well as resistance to the attack of thrips and various diseases that cause onion losses.

Henry A. Jones says it best in *Hybrid Onions:* "Onion losses cannot be entirely prevented but they can be greatly reduced by selecting the best adapted varieties and then following the best known cultural practices" (p. 3). If you're unsure about the best varieties for your area and don't know which cultural practice is best, seek out one of these bureaus or agencies; the information is free for the asking.

STARTING YOUR CROP FROM SEED

Starting your crop from seed is a somewhat risky and tedious business. Although starting your crop from seed is the most economical method of growing onions, it is also the least popular because it takes so much longer to produce a crop. However, with this method you can have a greater selection of varieties, and you can be more certain that the onion you are growing is the one you wanted in the first place.

This may not always hold true with sets or plants, particularly if you are buying from a self-service nursery or store. Not that the dealer is dishonest, but some customers are careless. They pick up a bundle of onion plants or a handful of sets, then decide they don't want them after all and toss them back in the bin. Which bin? A bunch of Bermuda onion plants or sets looks pretty much like any other variety of onion plants or sets, but there's a great deal of difference in their hardiness and keeping quality.

Although under proper conditions onion seeds germinate quickly, in six to ten days, success is also contingent on a number of other factors. Seeds require a germination temperature of around 68° F., and moisture must be controlled carefully, both during germination and after seedlings emerge. Too much moisture, particularly during the night, can lead to damping-off, which may wipe out the entire planting. On one day you will see the tender green shoots rising from the soil, erect and apparently healthy, and the next time you check on their progress the plants will literally have disappeared! (This disease and its control are described more fully in chapter 5.)

The ideal temperature for onion seedlings is 54–68° F., and it takes eight to ten weeks, or longer, to produce plants large enough for setting in the garden. When onions are to be seeded directly into the rows where the plants are to grow, temperature must be taken into consideration, because onions are very temperamental; they seem to have their own built-in thermostat. The seeds will not germinate unless temperatures are right, and this same temperamental streak rules their behavior right through to the harvest.

When seeded directly in the garden, the seeds are planted about one-half to one inch deep, and spaced about four or five seeds to an inch. This will assure a good stand and will provide extra plants for filling in if some of the seeds fail to germinate. When seedlings are established, thinning should begin, but not too drastically at first, until you see how they're coming along. At last thinning, the plants should stand three to four inches apart in the row.

Many writers tell us that the viability of onion seed is short—usually no more than two years. However, this may be a case of simply repeating what others have written. (I hate to admit it, but I too have been guilty of publishing this statement; I had read it so often, I believed it to be true.) But according to the USDA, onion seeds remain viable for years if handled properly. Victor R. Boswell, in "What Seeds Are and Do," has this to say: "Onion seeds kept in a warm, humid place will lose their life in a few months. When they are well dried and sealed in glass, they remain viable more than a dozen years at room temperature. If seeds are relatively dry, most kinds will tolerate for years extreme cold that would quickly kill their parent plants" (p. 1). As chief of the Vegetable and Ornamentals Research Branch of the USDA Agricultural Research Service, Boswell was in a position to know.

Some gardeners deliberately allow a few seed stalks to form, with seed production in mind. This is one way of being sure of viable seed when planting time comes around again. But remember, if the variety is a hybrid, seed saving is not advisable because the next generation of plants will not be the same as the one from which you're harvesting the seeds, or they may not be fertile at all (see chapter 1). Instead of saving the seeds, why not plant them? Of course, they must be from a standard open-pollinated variety. Except in extreme winter regions, onion seed can be planted in late August or even into September for an extra-early crop in the spring.

Plant as usual, and if seedlings come up thickly, let them grow. You can do your thinning in the spring, when plants will be needed for other rows.

When it's time for winter to move in, mulch the area with two or three inches of hay or other suitable material until freezing weather and snows are gone. When spring thaws come, remove the mulch and plants will soon be vigorously growing again. By wintering them over in the ground, northern gardeners have quite a jump on the season.

In the mild-winter regions of the South, growth will not be halted, so instead of covering the plants with mulch the seedlings are allowed to grow on to transplanting size, then thinned out and set into rows, where they will continue to grow throughout the winter to be harvested in the spring.

GROWING YOUR ONION CROP FROM SETS

My Hoosier grandmother used to say that nothing chased the gloom of an Indiana winter like the sight of onion sets in spring. What matter if wintry winds continued to whistle over frozen meadows, or if snow still lurked behind hedgerows and in fence corners? When those small, plump bulbs of white, red, or yellow appeared in shop displays she knew that the ground would soon be thawing, and planting time was drawing near.

There are both advantages and disadvantages to growing the onion crop from sets instead of seeds. The sets cost more, but they are a much surer path to take when you consider the many perils that can threaten a crop started from seed: poor germination, damping-off, and so on. And, sets entail less work. When sets are used, no thinning or transplanting is required. The bulbs are simply pressed into the soil at the proper spacing and allowed to grow. Another great advantage, particularly for the gardener whose growing season is short, is that an onion crop started from sets will have time to mature when it would be impossible from seeds. These sets already have a season's development behind them, and as soon as conditions are right to break their dormancy, they will burst into growth again.

One drawback to using this method is that onion sets may be carriers of nematodes and diseases that were present in the soil where the sets were grown. If they are carriers, your soil will become contaminated too. The best way to avoid this is to grow your own sets.

To produce sets, onion seed is sown thickly in a special bed, preferably in light, poor soil. Being crowded and having little nourishment prevents the bulbs from growing large and causes premature ripening. The foliage will eventually die back, as with the regular onion crop. When this happens, the sets are harvested, cured, and stored in a cool, dry place for the next season's use.

Onion sets are widely used in the Midwest and the North, but

The Early Harvest onions on the left were direct-seeded, while those on the right were grown from transplants. Direct seeding is the most economical method of growing onions; however, because of the equal spacing, transplants produce more attractive bulbs of uniform size and shape. Courtesy Dessert Seed Co.

unless a source for adapted varieties can be found, they are not practical for spring planting in the South except when they are intended for use as green onions. The varieties that are available as sets from mail order catalogs—usually Ebenezer and Danvers (but more often labeled simply as yellow or white)—are not adapted to the long hot summers of the Gulf Coast region.

Sets are sometimes used for fall planting in those areas, however, as they grow through the winter and produce large, dry onions in the spring. These sets are usually purchased from a local supplier, who makes it a point to furnish varieties that do well in the area.

The depth for planting onion sets is determined by the texture of the soil. In heavy-textured soils, the bulbs are merely pressed into the earth and barely covered, but in light soils they are planted deeper. The usual spacing is three to four inches apart.

In *Ruth Stout's No-Work Gardening Book,* Stout and Richard Clemence describe an even easier method of planting onion sets. The sets are simply scattered on the ground or on last year's mulch and covered with hay. Stout claims that some of her onions grow to a pound and a half, so her system must work!

The preferred size for onion sets is one-half to three-quarters of an inch in diameter if they are to be grown as a bulb crop. Larger sets produce eating-sized green onions more quickly; however they must be pulled promptly or they may form seed stalks.

It is well to take set size into consideration at planting time and to alternate the large and small sets in the row, so that thinnings used for green onions will be the ones with a tendency to bolt. If too many large sets are planted close together, long gaps may be left in the row. Another procedure might be to plant all the large sets in a section away from the bulb crop, with a harvest of green onions in mind.

If seed stalks do form on the plants grown for bulbs, they should be broken off immediately, or else the whole strength of the plant will go speedily to the formation of seeds instead of to the growth of the bulb. If allowed to ripen, these seed stems form a hard core in the center of the onion bulb and may cause the onion to rot in storage.

If you have a youngster in your family, why not buy a pint or so of onion sets for a children's garden this year? Onion sets are ideal subjects for such a project; they are eager to grow, and young gardeners are delighted at the sight of the first green shoots poking through the ground. If sets are planted at the right time, they will quickly reward your youngster with strong, vigorous seedlings, and will provide you with a bountiful harvest of onions.

Who knows? Such a venture could lead to horticultural greatness, if not to the making of another Kolreuter or Mendel, at least to the heart of a gardener who finds joy in the sight of onion sets in spring.

GROWING ONIONS FROM TRANSPLANTS

The trend toward using transplants instead of sets or seeds has been gaining in popularity with gardeners all across the country.

Each year, thousands of carefully graded plants are shipped from Texas and other southern growing regions to fill the demand at garden centers, local seed stores, mail-order houses, and from home gardeners everywhere.

When garden planting time rolls around, you can pick up almost any farm or garden publication and find notice of onion plants for sale. The plants are usually offered in lots of three-hundred or more, sometimes in individual bunches of seventy-five to one-hundred. The price varies according to the variety and the grower. Shipping to the southern states begins in late December and continues to the northern regions through June.

Some gardeners claim that larger-sized bulbs can be produced if onions are started from young transplants instead of sets. This is generally true, but perhaps not for the reason most people think.

Bermuda, Spanish, Grano, and Granex, all of which are large-bulb varieties, are the only ones usually available as plants. On the other hand, Ebenezer, Globe varieties, and Red Wethersfield are generally favored for the production of dry sets. Most gardeners choose a yellow or white onion for their main crop, and since both Ebenezer and Globe types produce medium-sized bulbs, it stands to reason that onions produced from these will not attain the size of the large-type varieties.

Many gardeners, in order to have an alternate choice of varieties, prefer to grow their own transplants. This is usually done by preparing a raised seedbed, with finely pulverized soil that is free from old crop residues, rocks, and the like. When the soil has been raked smooth and leveled, seed is planted in shallow drills four to six inches apart, or broadcast over the surface. Whichever method is used, care should be taken to allow at least an inch between the seeds. If spaced too closely, the plants will be spindly, and weeding will be difficult.

This seedbed should not be located in an area where onions have grown for at least four or five years, because many of the fungus diseases affecting onions remain in the soil long after the crop has been harvested.

The pink root fungus in particular can spell disaster for the onion crop. If the soil is contaminated with this fungus, not only will the seedlings be affected but spores of the fungus will be carried on their roots, infecting the soil of the transplanting area. (Pink root is discussed in chapter 5.)

While it is true that diseases such as this as well as damage from insects may pose a threat to the onion crop, an even worse enemy is weeds. The battle begins with the preparation of the seedbed and continues throughout the growing season.

As the soil is cultivated, weed seeds are brought to the surface, where they germinate quickly. Whereas onion seeds take seven to ten days to make an appearance, weeds seem to shoot up overnight. If they are allowed to remain in the seedbed, their rapid growth will choke out the onions in a very short time.

Onions need light to grow properly, and weeds not only will shade the plants but will rob them of soil nutrients and moisture. Even after transplanting, weeds must be kept in control, but it is especially important at this crucial stage, when the young seedlings are making their first growth.

Commercial growers use herbicides for weed control. They spray the ground before the onion seed is planted and thereby destroy the weeds before the seeds have a chance to germinate. Ecology-minded home gardeners favor hand weeding and the hoe. If weeds are pulled out while they are small, they are easily removed, and there is very little disturbance to the roots of the onions.

For onions being grown for family use only, say, in no more than one-hundred to three-hundred feet, a container for the seedbed may be used. My favorite for this purpose is an old washtub. It will hold, without crowding, all the onion transplants we need for our kitchen garden. If two or more varieties of seeds are being planted, the tub's surface is sectioned off by inserting division markers between the sections. The markers I use are cut from horizontal strips of fiber-glass left over from building greenhouses. Because it's corrugated, the material is quite firm and presses easily into the planting medium. Strips cut from bleach bottles would serve the same purpose.

Because the tub is filled with a sterile medium, there are no weed seeds to sprout, and I find it much easier to control the moisture, plus I know the plants will be safe from soil-borne diseases.

Here in the South, we can leave our onion tub outside throughout the winter, covering it only if a blue norther is due during the early stages of growth. After plants are well established, they are hardy enough to survive our winters.

Besides having a choice of varieties, and the money I save, there are other reasons why I prefer to grow my own transplants from seed. When I buy plants—whether from a local dealer or by mail order—how do I know they were not started on fungus-infested soil? Another drawback to buying plants is the matter of plant pruning. To conserve space and expense in shipping, commercial growers trim both roots and tops from the plants, leaving about an inch of root and tops that are five or six inches in length. According to Jones and Mann *(Onions and Their Allies)*, such pruning reduces the yield. Jones reports a five-year test on the effect of pruning that he and G. N. Davis conducted in California.

Five varieties of onions were tested: California Early Red, Stockton Yellow Globe, Red 21, San Joaquin, and Crystal Grano. At transplanting time three methods of pruning were applied: (1) roots were pruned, (2) tops were pruned, or (3) both roots and tops were pruned. At the end of each growing period, yield of mature bulbs was measured against the yield of plants that had no pruning: "A considerable reduction in yield occurred when both tops and roots were pruned, but the reduction was not always statistically significant. Root pruning seemed to be less damaging than top pruning, but neither was as detrimental as pruning both the tops and roots" (p. 118). Until I read Jones' report on these tests, I had trimmed the roots and tops of my plants as a matter of course. After all, that's the way the experts—the commercial growers, who certainly knew more about producing onions than I did—did it. And pruning did make them a lot easier to plant; all you did was poke a hole in the ground, stick the plants in, firm the soil, and give them a drink of water.

Now my onions are planted with roots and tops intact, just as they grew in the seedbed. Before lifting them from the seedbed, I make a furrow in the garden, one that is deep enough to allow spreading of the untrimmed roots. Then I lay the seedlings in a slanting position, like pencils all leaning in the same direction against one side of the furrow and spaced about four inches apart. As quickly as possible, to prevent drying out, I cover the roots with soil from the other side.

When all the plants are in place, I use a garden rake to close in the furrow by drawing the soil from first one side of the row, then the other. By raking the soil from the "tops side" first, drawing the soil close to their base, I bring the plants into an upright position. Soil raked in from the other side finishes covering the roots.

When transplanting almost any other type of plant in the garden, I "puddle" the roots in with water, firming the soil as I go. With onions, I set all the plants first and, without firming the soil, I turn on the sprinklers. The water, filtering down through the surface, distributes fine soil particles around the feeder roots in a far more natural manner than I can do by hand.

Seedlings transplanted with this method show little, if any, sign of setback. And Jones was right: onions planted without pruning do yield a better harvest.

When Henry Jones speaks, home gardeners would do well to listen, for he probably knows more about onions than anyone else on earth. If you can beg, borrow, or buy a copy of *Onions and Their Allies*, you will find it to be the most enlightening volume on the subject you have ever read.

HARVESTING AND STORING THE ONION CROP

As days grow longer and temperatures begin to climb, the built-in thermostat that even before germination of the seed has been directing the onion's development once again dictates the course that it must take.

The time of maturity is drawing near. Leaves and roots cease to grow, and the food still present in the leaves moves down into the bulb. The bulb, responding eagerly to this unprecedented feast, grows fat and succulent and soon begins pushing its plump shoulders through the soil.

The tops of the plants, now divested of nutrients to keep them

Table 4. Varieties for Specific Uses
GREEN (BUNCHING) ONIONS

Evergreen Bunching Onion	Long White Shank	Beltsville Bunching Onion
White Sweet Spanish Valencia	White Lisbon	Southport White Globe
Stokes Early Mild Bunching O.	Long White Globe	Long White Tokyo
Crystal White Wax	Portugal	Hardy White Bunching
Louisiana Pearl Shallots	Prosperity	Bayou Pearl Shallots
Louisiana Evergreen Shallots	Potato Onion	Delta Giand Shallots
Egyptian Onion	Welsh Onion	Hi-Shi-Ko

FOR PICKLING	FOR DEHYDRATION	TO GROW SETS
Yellow Ebenezer	Southport White Globe	Australian Brown
White Ebenezer	White Creole	White Ebenezer
Silver Queen	Primero	Red Wethersfield
Pickle Pak F_1	Creoso	Yellow Ebenezer
Regina	Dehyso	Stuttgarter
White Portugal	Dehydrator No. 2	White Portugal
Barletta	Dehydrator No. 4	Golden Mosque
Rakkyo	Dehydrator No. 6	
	Dehydrator No. 7	
	Dehydrator No. 8	
	Dehydrator No. 14	

ONION PLANTS (Named varieties usually listed in catalogs)	ONION SETS (Named varieties usually listed in catalogs)	ONION SETS (Usually available only from specialty growers)
Yellow Sweet Spanish	Yellow Globe Danvers	Potato Onions
White Sweet Spanish	Yellow Ebenezer	Egyptian Onions
Crystal White Wax	White Ebenezer	Catawissa Onions
Red Wethersfield	Stuttgarter	French Shallots
Hybrid Yellow Spanish		Oriental Chives
Hybrid Bermuda		Common Chives
		Siberian Chives
		Elephant Garlic
		Rocambole

alive, begin to turn brown and die. Even before they have turned all the way, the tissue of the neck area just above the bulb becomes weakened, and eventually the browned tops fall to the ground.

In the North, onions are dug when all the leaves have fallen, but the usual practice in the South is to harvest when 30 to 40 percent of the leaves are dead. If harvested any sooner the neck area will not have softened sufficiently to allow shrinkage, and bacteria will enter, causing the center of the bulb to rot.

Some gardeners contend that it's best to hasten this "dying" process by bending all the leaves over by hand, usually with the back of a rake. Their theory is that all the plant's strength will be directed to the bulb, thereby producing larger onions. Others insist that breaking the stems in this manner allows moisture to enter the bulb, shortening storage life. (I cast my vote with the latter.)

I'm a strong believer in the wisdom of nature when it comes to dragging a rake across the tops of my onions. Nature's way is to allow the leaves to ripen slowly, finishing their work before they fall. So long as tops are standing, the plant is still in its growth cycle. Why hasten its demise?

But even more important is the potential danger of losing a good part, if not all, of the storage crop to a parasite named *Botrytis allii*, more commonly known as neck rot. If the tops are bent over while still green, especially when a rake is used, the protective membrane of the neck is broken, leaving a wound that is ideal for penetration and infection by this parasite and other decaying organisms.

A far safer way of producing extra-large onions is by gradually drawing the soil away from the bulb, leaving only the roots in the ground during the final stages of growth. According to the old-timers, this method not only produces large, sound onions, but is a sure way of avoiding "scullions"—onions whose necks remain thick and green right up to harvest, instead of drying and shrinking in the usual way.

I've tried all three methods and am inclined to agree with the old-timers. Besides producing larger onions, and no scullions, there are other advantages to this method. Bulbs are already partially dry by harvest time, and harvesting itself is easier. With a slight tug, the bulbs are out of the ground, clean, soil-free, ready for curing.

Also to be considered is the possibility of a prolonged rainy period during this critical time of growth. Bulbs that have not been uncovered are more likely to be damaged by rotting than those that are exposed to air.

If the old-timers' method is used, soil removal should begin when the leaves begin to brown. And it should be done very gradually, to allow the skin and outer scales to "toughen." The soil serves as a protective blanket around the bulb; if it is removed too abruptly, the tender outer scales have a tendency to burst.

Bulbs at this stage are also susceptible to an injury called sunscald. This is particularly true in the South, where solar rays can become torrid, even early in the spring. A light mulch or other form of shade to protect bulbs from afternoon sun usually guards against this injury. (See chapter 5.)

When the weather is dry at harvest time, most gardeners leave the onions lying in the open to cure for a day or two before bringing them inside. It should be remembered that during this curing process all onions, particularly the white varieties, are subject to sunscald. To avoid such damage, bulbs should be protected from direct exposure to the sun. This is usually done by a method known as "shingling," in which the onions are pulled with their tops intact and placed in bunches along the row so that the leaves of each bunch cover the bulbs of the previous bunch.

After this initial curing, the onions are spread out in a dry, well-ventilated area for a couple of weeks to finish curing before storing. When tops are shriveled and dry, they should be cut off, leaving one inch of stem on the bulb. The tops may be left on small onions, to be braided so the onions can be hung in storage. Large bulbs are usually stored in slatted crates or mesh bags.

Care should be taken not to bruise or damage the bulbs at any stage, as this makes them susceptible to bacterial or fungus infections, which may attack after they are placed in storage. If damage has occurred, the blemished bulbs should be stored separately and used as soon as possible. The same is true of scullions if they are present, because their storage life is short.

These onions for dehydration are laid out for an annual field-day inspection. Courtesy Dessert Seed Co.

The ideal storage temperature for onions is 32°, with humidity at 60 to 70 percent. Most of us, however, cannot supply these ideal cold storage conditions and must rely instead on dry, well-ventilated attics or other unheated rooms.

Variable weather conditions outside may also cause temperatures inside our storage room to fluctuate. A prolonged high temperature can cause sprouting; if temperatures dip too low, the bulbs in storage may freeze. This doesn't happen too often, but if it should, the frozen bulbs should not be handled or moved until they are completely thawed. A slight freeze will not hurt them.

Nor will the formation of sprouts damage the bulbs if they are used within a reasonable length of time. This is nature's message that the bulb is ready to start growing again. The same built-in thermostat that has influenced the plant's progress from germination of the seed, growth of the plant, to maturity of the bulb now marks its eagerness to enter the next phase—the production of seed of its own kind, beginning the life cycle all over again.

Red, yellow, brown, or white—it's no wonder the common onion has become known through the ages as a culinary jewel!

COMMON NAMES ARE CONFUSING

Judging from the number of inquiries we received at the herb farm, home gardeners are more confused about onions, particularly multiplying onions, than about any other herb or vegetable that grows. Part of this confusion stems from the fact that practically every member of the *Allium* family would be a multiplier if allowed to remain in place.

Several varieties are called multiplier onions. They're also known by more than a dozen other common names: winter onion, top onion, tree onion, Egyptian onion, potato onion, cluster onion, bunching onion, Welsh onion, shallot, among others. Sometimes they're even referred to as scallions. This use of common names, plus changes in nomenclature through the years, has caused a great deal of bewilderment among gardeners.

The potato onion, for example, was first classified in 1827 by George Don, who gave it the botanical name *Allium cepa* variety *aggregatum* (the correct name). Later another botanist named Freidrich Alefield, who thought he'd found it first, called it *A. c.* var. *solaninum*. Then along came L. H. Bailey, who described it as *A. c.* var. *multiplicans.*

The same circumstances were true of the variety commonly referred to as Egyptian onion. Before *Hortus Third, A. cepa* var. *viviparum* was considered the valid name and was credited to F. Alefield, who found it first. *A. c. bulbelliferum* was the name given it by Bailey, whose work came later. *A. c. proliferum* is the name bestowed on the plant by Targioni-Tozzetti.

In both cases, three botanists in different places named the plant, not knowing it was being classified by another. This explains the contradictions found in various reference books.

To add to the confusion, the potato onion has many other common names: ground onion, underground onion, hill onion, election day onion, red multiplier, old-fashioned multiplier and Egyptian onion.

Egyptian Onion which botanists knew as *A. cepa* var. *viviparum* becomes an enigma on its own. It is also known as tree onion, top onion, walking onion, multiplier onion, even potato onion!

37

With these two masquerading under each other's aliases, it's no wonder gardeners are puzzled. And the many, many hybrids that have appeared through the years as a result of crossbreeding the different species and producing varieties that resemble one or the other (or both) baffle understanding even more.

Botanical names may seem of little consequence to the average home gardener, who simply wishes to grow onions for the family table, but they are of utmost importance to those who wish to grow a specific kind. We wouldn't think of going into a metropolis and inquiring where to find Slim or Shortie if a man named James Harrison McIntyre was the one person we were looking for.

So it is in the plant world. When you order a variety by a nickname or common name—multiplying onions, for example— you may end up with potato onions, Egyptian onions, Welsh onions, ever-ready onions, shallots, or rakkyo, an Asian variety you've never even heard of.

All onions will multiply, even the common onion, although it is not generally thought of as a multiplier because the bulbs are harvested as soon as they mature. But it will multiply, if given a chance. If you don't believe it, try planting one of the large bulbs and see what happens. (This is a good way to dispose of onions that have sprouted in the storage bin.) When temperatures are cool enough to break their dormancy, and moisture is supplied, the bulb will send up numerous green shoots, and the harvest will be several bulbs from one onion. These green shoots are delicious when added to salads.

The names "scallions" and "bunching onions" add to the onion confusion. Neither of these is a variety, yet a season seldom passed at the herb farm that we didn't have customers requesting them, in the belief that they were a type of multiplying onion.

A scallion is simply a green onion, one that is pulled before the bulbs mature. It may be a young plant of any onion variety: Egyptian onion, potato onion, Welsh onion, shallot. Often the common onion crop is planted with a harvest of scallions in mind. The sets or plants are spaced two or three inches apart in the row, and every other one is harvested green, leaving the rest to mature.

Home gardeners sometimes refer to multiplying onions as bunching onions because the plants grow in bunches or clusters. But when a commercial grower uses that term, he or she is talking about green onions that are tied up in bunches for market, like the ones you find in the produce section at the grocery store. If you're the type who likes to experiment "just to see what happens," try planting a few green onions from the produce section in your grocery store. Potato onions, Egyptian onions, Welsh onions, and shallots are all favored varieties for producing green onions. This might be one way of getting a start of a multiplying variety. But of course you must also realize that the common onion is also sometimes grown (though on a lesser scale) for the production of bunching onions for market.

Shallot is another common name that may result in a crop that is disappointing, if not to the gardener at least to the cook. The true French shallot has a flavor all its own, and most of the shallots offered for sale in the United States are *Allium cepa* cultivars: multiplying forms arrived at by crossing the common onion with a multiplying variety such as Welsh onion. Or, they may be crosses between the cultivars themselves.

Not that there's anything wrong with commercially cultivated shallots; they produce mild-flavored bulbs that are regarded as favorites by many gardeners and cooks. But if it's the true French shallot you're seeking—the *eschalot* of the *haute cuisine* of France—order your bulbs by botanical name, *Allium ascalonicum*, and hope for the best. The true French shallot is extremely hard to find.

Be it shallots, potato onions, gooseberries, or whatever, there is only one valid botanical name for a particular plant, and it is the same throughout the world. Common names vary from region to region, and from country to country, but botanical names remain the same. If you know this name, you can order with confidence from any nursery or from any country, whether you speak the language or not.

RELATIVES OF THE COMMON ONION

The genus *Allium* is large. Through the years more than a thousand names for the various species have been proposed, but modern botanists now conclude that about half of these are synonyms. Cases in point are the potato onion and the Egyptian onion. The potato onion has been known under three botanical names: *Allium cepa* variety *aggregatum, A. c.* var. *solanicum,* and *A. c.* var. *multiplicans.* Only the first is right. This is the name given the plant in 1827 by George Don, who was the first botanist to classify it. The other two are names applied by later botanists, and therefore synonyms.

With the publication of Bailey's *Hortus Third,* the new standard plant reference, the potato onion has undergone yet another modification in its botanical identification. Granted, the change is very slight, having to do only with the way the botanical name is written, not in the name itself. But even this variation will be confusing to many gardeners who are making a serious effort to classify plants botanically. Heretofore, the valid name for the potato onion was written in this manner: *Allium cepa* variety *aggregatum.* Now the plant is identified simply as *A. cepa,* Aggregatum Group.

And Egyptian onion, the pride of many gardens, which hundreds of writers (and gardeners) have fondly labeled *A. cepa* var. *viviparum,* must now accept the cold, impersonal classification *A. cepa,* Proliferum Group. (So it shall be in any books that I write, but in my heart and in my garden this beauty will always be the fascinating *viviparum!*)

Personally, I like the old classification best, the designating of each family member by its own botanical name. In this regard, plants and people are a lot alike, and without an identifying name many of the old favorites may get lost in the shuffle. For instance, I have relatives in my home state of Indiana and in Ohio, Illinois, Montana, and California. Much as I love my adopted state of Texas, I wouldn't want this state to be my only means of identification. Considering the number of family members who moved here with me, or who followed me, with no more identification than *Coonse clan,* Texas Group, any one of us would be pretty hard to find. This may also hold true with specific varieties of onions.

But who am I to question the wisdom of the authors of a monumental work such as *Hortus Third?* Liberty Hyde Bailey and his daughter Ethel Zoe Bailey initially compiled the material that went into this volume; their program of research began before the turn of the century. For more than two decades before its publication, the staff of the L. H. Bailey Hortorium at Cornell University revised and expanded the entries to reflect current knowledge and conceptual changes that had occurred over the past thirty-five years and to omit entries that had become obsolete, such as the numerous synonyms so prevalent in the *Allium* family.

A. cepa perutile is one such omission. "Exclusion" would be a better word, because as far as I've been able to determine, the name *perutile* has never appeared in *Hortus.* Yet, the ever-ready onion, listed under that name, has found its way into numerous encyclopedias and reference books. In most cases, the common name, buried on a list, is all that is given, and with good reason, for very little reference material is available on this particular onion. (See ever-ready onion in chapter 3.)

Of the four hundred or more *Allium* species recognized by *Hortus Third,* only seven are commonly regarded as food. However, there are forms or groups within some species that increase the edible number that are generally grown under cultivation. These are known as varieties.

Do not allow the word "variety" as it is used here to confuse you. Generally, when we use the word we are referring to a certain type of onion—Ebenezer, Bermuda, sweet Spanish, or any one of the hundreds of cultivars that have been introduced since hybridization began. In this instance, the word is used to designate the forms within the groups.

For example, the potato onion, ever-ready onion, Egyptian onion, and shallots are all forms of the common onion horticultural group. Yet, at the same time, they each have their individual character, which sets them apart from the common onion, and from each other. It is for this reason that each variety is given its own botanical name.

The classification that seems to create the most confusion has to do with shallots, particularly the one known as the true French shallot. This is the one that all of France and gourmet cooks throughout the world swear by as having superior flavor. It has almost lost its identity! Not that the plant doesn't still exist—it does. But its botanical classification *Allium ascalonicum* is now being shared by all commercially cultivated shallots, when in truth these commercial varieties are crosses between various multiplying types of onions and the common onion. According to *Hortus Third,* the original variety, which had been designated by France and all the world to be the true French shallot, was of uncertain origin.

Hortus Third has this to say about *A. ascalonicum:*

> ascalonicum: a confused name used by Linnaeous for what was probably a cultigen, though said to be native to Asia Minor. The name has been applied to the shallot, now considered to belong to the Aggregatum Group of *A. cepa,* but seeds or other material offered as *A. ascalonicum* sometimes prove to be other spp. The true shallot rarely flowers or sets seed. (p. 48)

The following list includes the seven species and the horticultural groups within the species that are commonly grown for food:

I. *Allium cepa* (3 groups)
   1. The *Cepa* Group
      Common onion
   2. The *Aggregatum* Group
      Ever-ready onion
      Shallot
      Potato onion
   3. The *Proliferum* Group
      Egyptian onion
      Catawissa onion
II. *Allium fistulosum*
   Welsh onion

III. *Allium Schoenoprasum*
    Chives
IV. *Allium tuberosum*
    Chinese chives
V. *Allium chinense*
    Rakkyo
VI. *Allium sativum*
    Garlic (common)
    Rocambole
VII. *Allium Ampeloprasum* (3 groups)
    1. The *Ampeloprasum* Group
      Great-headed garlic
    2. The *Porrum* Group
      Leek
    3. The *Kurrat* Group
      Kurrat

Bear in mind that the foregoing list includes only the basic ancestral species commonly cultivated in the *Allium* plant family; you
might call them the patriarchs of their species. This does not include the many near-relatives of those listed.

Common chives, for example, are credited with two near relatives: Oriental chives (*A. S.* variety *orientale*) and Siberian chives
(*A. S.* var. *sibiricum*). There are others—leeks, garlics, and so on—
and the list does not take into consideration the hundreds of cultivars that have descended from these venerable ancestors. A full
account of these descendants could fill a volume of its own.

To those of us who did not make the honor roll in foreign languages, the botanical names on the preceding list may not come
easy. But, easy or not, they are all we've got, for Greek and Latin
were the universal languages centuries ago, when these plants were
named.

The name *Allium* is taken from *all*, the Celtic word for pungent. *Cepa* comes from the Greek word *cepha*, meaning having a
head or headlike part. *Fistulosum* is also of Latin origin—*fistulosus*
means tubelike or tubular. *Proliferum* is almost self-explanatory; it
comes from a Latin word of Medieval times meaning prolific or

fertile. *Tuberosum* derives from the Latin word *tuberosus,* meaning knobby. (If you doubt this one, dig up a plant of Chinese chives and examine the root.) *Ampeloprasum,* it is said, was named for Ampelos, a Greek god who was placed among the stars by Dionysus. Jones and Mann, however, offer a more logical explanation in *Onions and Their Allies. Ampelos* means grapevine; *prason* means leek; a species found in vineyards. When you see the word *sativum,* as in garlic, it means that the plant is cultivated as a crop plant.

Far be it from me to try to convince you (or anyone else) that Latin is an easy language. The truth is, even in high school, I side-stepped the subject as though it were a nest of rattlesnakes. But the time came when I needed at least a smidgen of this information; you can't be a well-informed gardener without it. And certainly you cannot operate a nursery, such as became my lot when we started the Yankee Peddler Herb Farm. How glad I was then that I had learned the Latin names, because many of our orders did not come by common name, but by the scientific botanical names as they were known the world around. Remember the reference to Slim and Shortie?

While its true that Latin names are also confusing and difficult to pronounce at first, they do come easier as time goes on. All at once you realize that a good number of Latin names are close to their English counterparts, not only in spelling, but in pronunciation and meaning as well.

Take the word *aggregatum* of the *Allium cepa,* Aggregatum Group. Our English dictionary tells us that the word aggregate means "to collect or bring together; gather together in a mass or body." Knowing this, it is easily understood that the word in botanical language would translate the same. Potato onion, everready onion, and shallot all produce their bulbs in a mass or body.

Learning to write the word in Latin comes fairly easily; it's the pronunciation, the not knowing where to place the emphasis in speaking, that scares off most gardeners. The two rules that follow, though far from being conclusive, should be of help in pronouncing botanical names of the *Allium* family.

1. Words of two syllables are accented on the first: *ce'pa* (SEE·puh), *por'rum* (POR·rum).

2. Usually (though not always) words of more than two syllables are accented on the next-to-the-last syllable if the vowel in that syllable has a long sound: *sat i'vum* (sat·TIE·vum). Otherwise, accent is placed on the second-from-the-last syllable: *pro lif' er um* (pro·LIF·er·um).

My advice is to plunge right in, using the best judgment you can. And, if you happen to say a name wrong, don't feel too bad. Chances are that nine listeners out of ten won't know the difference anyhow. I'm not advocating that you be haphazard in your efforts toward proper pronunciation of the Latin names, but don't let uncertainty keep you from trying.

You may find yourself being corrected by someone who knows the subject better than you. If so, don't be embarrassed or offended. Thank your informer and admit that you may be a better gardener than you are a Latin linguist. Listen closely to the proper pronunciation—repeating it aloud if the situation permits—and store the syllables in your memory bank for future withdrawal.

Short of taking a Latin course, I guess the best way to learn how to pronounce these time-honored names is to join a garden club. Listen to the speakers, absorb every unfamiliar sound and syllable. Jot the word down, underlining the syllables that are accented; you can check out the correct spelling later. Soon you will have mastered the scientific jargon, and these botanical names will roll as eloquently off your tongue as your own native English.

Chances are you're already familiar with many of them—achimenes, ajuga, chrysanthemum, coleus, delphinium, geranium, datura, dahlia. You've probably been speaking Latin for years and didn't know it!

3

Onions Every Home Gardener Should Know

~

ALLIUMS COMMONLY GROWN FOR FOOD

"Help! I'm going out of my mind from sheer confusion!" That plea of desperation was the opening line of a letter we received from a mail-order customer of the herb farm a while back . . . a plea that, I might add, was the final nudge I needed to get this book written.

"What's the difference between multiplier onions? Potato onions? Egyptian onions? What are scallions? How do you plant the different kinds? How do you tell them apart?"

I have answered such questions so often in the past that I welcome the opportunity to get the answers in print. Yet I am almost afraid to do so because no matter what I say about onions, there's sure to be a deluge of letters from gardeners who disagree.

Onions are probably the least written about of any vegetable or herb. Not that there aren't numerous pieces published on the subject; the trouble is, they all say the same thing, and the information is not complete.

When you get right down to it, what *is* the difference between the various kinds?

To answer that question and supply directions for growing the various species will require repetition of material touched on in other chapters. But bear with me, please . . . this work is intended as a handbook for gardeners, not a contender for the Nobel Prize in literature.

This chapter's chief purpose is to present as simply as possible in an easy-to-find sequence the different onion species and to tell how to recognize and grow them.

First, let's get the scallions, multiplier onions, and bunching onions out of the way, for none of these are varieties, as so many gardeners seem to think. These names are simply terms descriptive of the plants' use or growth.

SCALLION

As mentioned in chapter 2, a scallion is any onion that does not form a bulb, for example, leeks, shallots, and Welsh onions. Scallions are not limited to these varieties alone, however. The name is also given to onions that are harvested in the green stage when plants are eight to ten inches high, with stems about half an inch thick. Often the main onion crop is planted with a harvest of scallions in mind. The sets or plants are spaced two or three inches apart in the row, and every other plant harvested is green; the rest are left to mature.

MULTIPLIER ONIONS

It seems that every variety in the garden except the common onion may be called a multiplier. The common onion is usually harvested before multiplying begins. If there is any one species, however, that most authorities are referring to when they use the term "multiplier," they are usually speaking of the potato onion, *A. cepa*, Aggregatum Group.

BUNCHING ONIONS

There are two schools of thought on just what bunching onions are. One group, including commercial growers, claims they are plants that are harvested in the green stage (like scallions) and tied into bunches for marketing. Others insist that bunching onions are the bulbless types that grow in bunches (clusters)—perennial evergreen onions, Welsh onions, certain varieties of leeks, and so on. Both are right. Any type of onion may be bunched when pulled in the small bulbless stage.

THE SEVEN *ALLIUM* SPECIES COMMONLY GROWN FOR FOOD
To avoid confusion, it should be remembered that two of the species (*A. cepa* and *A. ampeloprasum*) comprise horticultural groups within the species. Do not regard these groups as different species, but simply as forms of the species.

Allium Cepa L.
This species has three horticultural groups: the *Cepa* Group, the *Aggregatum* Group, and the *Proliferum* Group.

The *Cepa* Group. Only one form is represented in the *Cepa* group, but this includes most of the cultivars produced through the years, and all of the commercially important bulbing onions.

One of the hardiest of vegetable plants, the **common onion** (*A. cepa* var. *cepa*) is a bulbous-rooted biennial. It is so familiar it needs little description. Two kinds are commonly grown: the pungently flavored American varieties, and the mildly flavored Spanish and Bermudas. Varying in shape from flat to globular to elongated, the bulb of the common onion is simple, not composed of cloves, like garlic. The common onion usually forms but a single bulb, consisting of a series of succulent, concentric layers. When the bulb reaches maturity, the outer scales become tough and papery. Plants are usually started from seed and as the bulb forms, it sends up a rosette of large cylindrical leaves, enclosing a flowering scape, which appears in spring. Flowers are greenish white and produced in globular umbels. (See chapters 1 and 2 for more complete information about this species and how to grow it.)

The *Aggregatum* Group. The *Aggregatum* Group comprises varieties that multiply freely: ever-ready onion, shallot, and potato onion. Propagation is by division and replanting of the underground bulbs.

The well-named multiplying **ever-ready onion** (*A. cepa*, Aggregatum Group) resembles the Welsh onion in appearance and growing habits, and is often erroneously given that name. Both are evergreen and perennial, producing scallionlike onions that grow in clusters. Propagation is always by division, because the ever-ready onion rarely flowers.

The ever-ready onion, which so many garden writers have erroneously designated as *A. cepa perutile*, is not a species, but a cultivar that came to us from England. The name in itself is valid; it is the manner in which it is written that causes the confusion.

A botanical listing of this onion might be written in any one of these ways, and all would be correct: (1) *Allium cepa* L. (Aggregatum Group) cv. Perutile; (2) *Allium cepa* L. (Aggregatum Group) 'Perutile'; or (3) *Allium cepa* L. cv. 'Perutile.' The first letter of a cultivar name is always capitalized, and cultivars are always designated by the word "cultivar" (or its abbreviation, cv.) preceding the cultivar name, *or* the name is enclosed in apostrophes.

Jones and Mann present useful information concerning this misnomer in *Onions and Their Allies*. In this quotation they are referring to an account written by W. T. Stearn:

> Stearn points out that the Welsh or Japanese Onion, once an important spring market onion in England, had almost passed out of cultivation by the start of the present century, and that its common name had been largely transferred to the ever-ready onion, a form of *A. cepa* having a similar habit. The ever-ready onion "resembles the biennial, large-bulbed forms of *A. cepa* in flower as in leaf section, but is of perennial and prolific growth, has a much narrower bulb and narrower leaves, a shorter flower-stalk and smaller umbel." Stearn gave the name 'Perutile' (meaning "very useful") to the cultivar grown by Mr. Clarence Elliot of Stevenage, England, and marketed by him as the Welsh or ever-ready onion. This cultivar has reddish bulb-coats and leaves scarcely 1 cm. wide by some 40 cm. long. The lower part of the 40 to 55 cm.-high scape is inflated, as is typical of *A. cepa*, but the plant rarely flowers. The plants are "increased by division, never by seeds"; a single bulb planted in March produced 10 or 12 bulbs by autumn. (p. 34)

The ever-ready onion is also known as winter onion and evergreen or everlasting onion. The scallionlike stalks can be harvested one or more at a time, as needed, and production will not be halted; clusters will continue to form as long as at least one plant is left in place to multiply. Plants are spaced six to eight inches apart in the row and are absolutely hardy, needing no protection even in northern winters.

Surely any onion with such qualifications should have a place in every garden: perennial, prolific, evergreen, year-round harvest! What more could an onion lover ask?

Most gardening books prior to the publication of *Hortus Third* list the **shallot** (*A. cepa* L., Aggregatum Group) under the botanical name *A. ascalonicum.* This was the name given the species back in the 1700s by Swedish botanist Carl von Linné, better known to the world as Linnaeus. When gardeners who are also gourmet cooks are able to locate this species, they look on the bulbs as true miracles of flavor that will lift their culinary efforts from the commonplace to the extraordinary!

Unfortunately, the true shallot—the *eschalot* of France—is almost a plant of the past, at least as far as availability in our country is concerned. Few U.S. seed companies even list shallots in their catalogs, and none that I have found specify the botanical variety. The shallots that are offered may be yellow, white, reddish, or brown. As mentioned in chapter 2, these are cultivars: commercial varieties obtained through crosses between Welsh onion or other multiplying types and the common onion.

There is but one company from which I would suggest trying to acquire a start of the real thing: Vilmorin in France. This is said to be the oldest seed company in the world, and their catalog lists a number of shallot varieties. There is a drawback, however; their catalog is printed in French, so unless you are a student of that language you will need a translator before you can place your order.

Different garden writers offer so many conflicting opinions regarding the color of the variety we've known as *A. ascalonicum* that I sometimes wonder which shallot *is* the real thing. No wonder *Hortus Third* and modern botanists relieved it of its ancient horticultural standing; they probably were wondering too!

In *Herbs for Every Garden*, Gertrude B. Foster describes "clusters of reddish-brown skinned bulblets which give us the delectable, sweet onion, slightly tinged with a breath of garlic. They are a little stronger than chives but more subtle than garlic" (p. 172). Surely, with all her experience in growing herbs and as editor of *The Herb Grower Magazine*, Gertrude B. Foster should know.

But what about Milo Miloradovich's *The Art of Cooking with Herbs and Spices*, the *pièce de résistance* of all herb books? She defines the color as gray! This author couldn't be wrong, not with the capability of writing a classic such as this!

Then there's Angelo M. Pellegrini (a native of Italy, now living in the United States), who writes with such authority about this elusive member of the *Allium* family that we could never disagree with him. In *The Food Lover's Garden*, he gives a most interesting account of his relentless search and eventual success in locating the genuine shallot. He describes the individual bulbs as "egg-shaped and about an inch and a half long. The skin was brownish tinged with purple" (p. 121).

Could it be that color, like beauty (or ugliness), is in the eye of the beholder?

The Royal Horticultural Society's *Encyclopedia of Gardening* offers some enlightenment on the subject:

> There are 2 or 3 varieties of Shallot, the old true Shallot being the best for most purposes. It is about the size of a small walnut but elongated and narrowed to a point, coppery-red near the base and lighter above, the foliage being green. It does not often run to seed and if thoroughly dried and properly stored keeps well, even until May or June. The Jersey Shallot is as large as a small onion, roundish, with a thin red skin all over, and the foliage is grey-green. (p. 1946)

Again referring to the findings of W. T. Stearn, Jones and Mann in *Onions and Their Allies* present this information:

> Stearn (1960) has finally set the matter straight by showing that the Linnean type of *A. ascalonicum* is a specimen of a wild Palestinian plant that has long been known under the name *A. hierochuntinum* Bois. This species is in no way related to the cultivated

shallot, and suggests that the confusing epithet *ascalonicum* be rejected. However this name is used, it cannot be applied to any cultivated plants that we know as shallots. Morphological and genetic evidence indicates clearly that the latter are forms of *A. cepa.* (p. 35)

If Stearn is right—and who would dare question his word if experts in the field such as Jones and Mann accept his findings— then these shallots we've been relishing as *A. ascalonicum* are imposters! 'Tis said that a rose by any other name would smell as sweet. Maybe a paraphrase of the old adage also holds true for shallots.

Shallots are the most prolific of all the multipliers, and easier to grow than onions. And they offer bonus by furnishing a plentiful supply of green onions while they are growing and, later, a bountiful crop of bulbs for drying and storing.

Since shallots seldom produce seed, they are usually propagated by division. The single bulbs are spaced six to eight inches apart in rows nine to twelve inches apart, with their tops even with the soil.

Shallots grow in clusters, sometimes producing up to a dozen bulbs from a single plant. As the plants mature, the enlarged bulbs rest above the ground with only the roots remaining in the soil. The leaves and the stems form a rosette around them. When the leaves have turned brown, the clumps are lifted, dried, and stored in the same way as onions.

They keep well in storage, and bulbs that are left over can be used for starting another crop. Like other members of the *Allium* family, shallots are quite hardy and can be planted in spring or fall.

The **potato onion** (*A. cepa.* L., Aggregatum Group) is another prolific member of the onion family, yet it is also one of the most difficult to find. Potato onions are not the best of keepers; therefore, very few nurseries carry them.

Unlike the Egyptian onion, whose name the potato onion sometimes bears, the potato onion does not produce bulbs at the top, and it makes no seed. In fact, it rarely flowers. It is propagated only by division of the underground bulbs. During growth, these bulbs produce offsets around the seed bulb in much the same manner as the potato.

Potato onion bulbs are up to three inches in diameter and about two inches thick, with a flavor that is stronger than most other onions. Each mature bulb multiplies into a cluster, with each cluster averaging from six to eight bulbs. Under favorable conditions, twice that number is not unusual.

The crop may be started in spring or fall, except in extremely cold climates, in which case, spring is the time for planting. In most areas of the United States, however, they can be planted in the fall if mulched during the coldest months.

Depending on size, the bulbs are set two to four inches deep, and at least eight inches apart to allow room for them to multiply. Both large and small bulbs should be planted; the small bulbs will grow into large bulbs for eating, and the large bulbs will produce offsets for starting the following year's crop.

Potato onions should be dug as soon as the tops begin to die. The bulbs keep better in storage if harvested while most of the top is still green. Some gardeners claim that rotting is minimized by storing the bulbs upside down, thus preventing moisture from collecting around the stem end and entering the bulb.

The perennial **Egyptian onion** (*A. cepa* L., Proliferum Group [*A. cepa* var. *viviparum*]) variety is also called tree onion and top onion. It resembles the common onion in appearance: fat, globular leaves, strong, upright stems reaching a height of two feet or more. But instead of a seed head, it develops clusters of small, dark red onions one-half to one inch in diameter at the top of the slender stalks.

As these top bulblets increase in size and number, their weight bends the stalk to the ground, where the bulblets quickly take root and form a new colony of plants.

When planted singly, the bulblets grow into large, copper-colored underground bulbs by the end of the season. But these bulbs, grown from bulblets, will not produce top bulbs until the second year.

Though the underground bulb is edible, it is very strong in flavor and is seldom used for culinary purposes. It is the top bulbs that are used in cooking and for propagation.

Egyptian onions may be planted anytime. The bulblets are

spaced about six inches apart and two inches deep. New plants can also be started by dividing the underground bulbs. Because they are perennial and not of a pervasive nature, Egyptian onions can grow on in the same spot for years.

A great deal of controversy exists over the Egyptian onion and the Catawissa onion. Some authorities contend that they are one and the same. Others disagree. I cast my vote with the latter.

The **Catawissa onion** (*A. cepa* L., Proliferum Group) is also known as walking onion and perennial tree onion. Like the Egyptian onion, this variety also produces clusters of bulblets in its flower head, but these are often much lighter in color and smaller than those of the variety we've always known as *A. cepa viviparum*. It also differs in that well-developed bulbs are not produced underground, as is the case with the Egyptian onion.

Catawissa onion plants grow in tufts, in the same manner as chives, and can be propagated by dividing the tufts or by planting the top bulbs. Plants are spaced six to eight inches apart.

This variety appears more vigorous in growth than the Egyptian onion. It often produces a mixture of flowers and bulblets at the top of its thirty-inch stems, which usually form a second tier or cluster above the first. Occasionally, even a third tier of green shoots and leaves will appear. It is this rather bizarre habit that gives it the name walking onion.

As with Egyptian onions, the stems bend under the weight of the clusters, and bulblets touching the ground quickly take root. These rooted clusters may be lifted and divided, and each plant will soon form into a clump.

At maturity, the tops die back and the bulbs enter into a state of rest until cool weather comes again.

Allium fistulosum L. There are no groups within this species (as with *A. cepa* and *A. ampeloprasum*); however, because it has been in cultivation since prehistoric times, this species has many cultivated forms.

The **Welsh onion** (*A. fistulosum* L.), also known as Japanese bunching onion, is usually listed by U.S. seedsmen as evergreen bunching onion. This perennial evergreen plant resembles chives in its manner of growth, but its leaves are more like those of the common onion. The leaves, however, are almost perfectly round, whereas those of the common onion are flattened on the upper (or inner) side. Instead of well-defined bulbs, the Welsh onion produces slender, scallionlike stalks that are only slightly enlarged at the base.

There are several types of Welsh onions, although only two—the white Welsh and Japan's nebuka type—are commonly grown in the United States.

Nebuka is not the name of a particular onion; the term refers to those types that characteristically develop long, white stalks for blanching. The evergreen bunching onion listed in most seed catalogs is a nebuka type. Extra-long, thick, silvery white stalks up to six inches can be produced if soil is hilled up around the plants.

The nebuka type is a favorite for green onion marketing, and a choice selection for home gardeners because it continues to produce as long as weather conditions are favorable.

Because of its resistance to various diseases, insects, and adverse climatic conditions, the Welsh onion has figured prominently in plant breeding. Numerous multiplying cultivars have come from crosses between this species and *A. cepa*.

These hybrids, commonly known as shallots, inherit two dominant characteristics of the Welsh onion: they are perennials, and they have the multiplying tendency of the Welsh onion. However, they also inherit a notable characteristic of the other parent, the common onion: instead of long, slender stalks like those of the Welsh onion, the hybrids produce a "nest" of small but well-defined bulbs at the base of the plant.

These plants, growing in clusters, can be harvested for use as green onions or allowed to develop into bulbs for storing. As the bulbs mature, the tops die back and the plants enter a stage of dormancy, as does the common onion.

Welsh onions are said to have originated in the Orient, but are now grown in most areas of the world. The name originated in Europe, not in Wales, as many writers claim.

Jones and Mann offer this explanation in *Onions and Their Allies:* "The name Welsh, suggesting that this onion may have originated in Wales, is possibly a corruption from the German 'welsche'—i.e. foreign—a name applied when this onion was introduced into Germany, probably at the end of the Middle Ages (Stearn, 1943). Stearn also adds that it has never been commonly grown in Wales" (pp. 78–79). Although the Welsh onion is adapted to all regions, there is no record of this species having grown in the wild. Propagation is by seed, or by division of the underground bulbs, with the plants spaced six to eight inches apart. Planting may be done in spring or fall.

Allium Schoenoprasum **L.** There are no groups within this species. However, according to Jones and Mann, few species are more variable both under cultivation and in the wild state.

Since hybridization may take place under ordinary garden conditions, this variation is of a continuous nature and changes from one generation to the next. Consequently, no effort has been made to classify the numerous chives. *Hortus Third* lists, along with the common chive, two other varieties: *orientale* and *sibiricum*. Both of these are wildlings. The first, var. *orientale*, is native to east Asia; var. *sibiricum* is native to both Siberia and North America.

Common chives (*A. Schoenoprasum* L.) are the smallest and most delicately flavored member of the onion tribe. They have been favorites since ancient times, not only in the kitchen but in the garden as well.

Widely used as an ornamental edging in herb gardens because of its neat, compact growth and attractive rosy purple flowers, this ten-inch-high, tufted perennial is equally at home in rock gardens and flower beds, or even in a pot on a sunny kitchen window sill where the succulent dark green leaves may be snipped as needed for seasoning salads, soups, and sauces.

In the garden, chives are completely hardy to cold, withstand drought, and are not fussy about the soil in which they're planted. In warm climates, they are evergreen, but in cold regions the leaves die back in late autumn, to reappear the next spring.

Although the entire plant is edible, it is chiefly for the tender, cylindrical leaves that chives are grown. To ensure a continuous supply, the leaves should be cut regularly (at least three or four times) during the growing season. If not needed for immediate use, the harvested leaves may be snipped with scissors into quarter-inch pieces and stored in airtight jars in the freezer.

The proper way to cut chives is just above the soil line. This not only stimulates growth of new leaves, but promotes multiplication of the bulbs as well. You should never cut just the tips of the leaves, for the cut will turn brown, and eventually the whole leaf will dry up and die.

Harvesting is usually less drastic when chives are grown on the kitchen window sill. Here, cutting is done almost daily, taking a few spears at a time for use in cooking. By always taking the long, outer leaves new leaves are continuously springing up from their shorn stems.

Chives grown indoors need at least a three- or four-inch pot, starting with eight to ten crowns per pot. When the plants seem crowded or roots begin showing at the bottom of the pot, it is time to remove them from the pot, divide the clusters, trim back the roots and the tops, and repot the crowns.

In the garden, chive plants should be divided every three or four years. This is done by lifting the clumps in spring and separating them into smaller clumps of five or six bulblets. These divisions are then reset in the garden, allowing about eight inches between them. With proper care, the plants will quickly multiply and fill in the empty spaces.

Although chives can be started from seed, it is a long wait— usually two years—before plants are large enough for harvest. For that reason, most gardeners start with plants. These are usually available at nurseries and produce markets early in the spring.

Like all members of the *Allium* family, chives grow best in a loose, friable soil that is rich in nutrients, especially nitrogen. Soil feeding is particularly needed right after the plants have been cut, to stimulate the growth of new leaves. Bone meal is always a good choice in the open garden, and liquid fertilizer, such as fish emulsion, is my first choice for potted chives. To keep plants producing well, nutrients should be applied about once a month.

Allium tuberosum **Rottler ex Sprengel.** There are no groups within the species.

It seems there has always been confusion in botanical literature about **Chinese chives** *(A. tuberosum)* and a closely related species, *A. ramosum,* commonly known as fragrant-flowered garlic. Both are native to southeastern Asia.

Both are very alike in their growing habits: elongated bulbs individually attached to a stout rhizome much like that of a common iris; flowering scapes about twenty inches high and bearing fragrant white starlike flowers; four to nine leaves per bulb; leaves one-eighth to five-sixteenth of an inch wide, shorter than the scape.

There are notable differences between the two, however whereas the leaves of fragrant-flowered garlic are slightly hollow and rounded on the back, those of Chinese chives are solid, flattish on the upper side, and slightly ridged below, like leeks and garlic, but they do not have the lengthwise fold found in leeks and garlic.

The flowering time is also different. Fragrant-flowered garlic blooms in early summer, Chinese chives in late summer. Although flowers of both species are fragrant, these plants, like all members of the *Allium* family, have the characteristic onion odor when any part of the plant is cut or crushed. And, like all members of the *Allium* family, both are edible (if you like the taste), but it is the one called Chinese chives that is valued in Asian cooking.

Also known as garlic chives and Oriental garlic, this is the *Allium* you want if you like a touch of garlic, but can't tolerate the pungent, overpowering taste of the real thing.

According to *Chinese Medicinal Herbs,* compiled and published by Li Shih-chen in 1578, the Chinese ate the whole plant. It was especially relished when in flower in midsummer. It was known as fêng pên (the rich root), and was used for sacrifices in the ancestral temple and for other sacrifices. In the Orient, the plant is valued not only as a food, but for its medicinal virtues as well. It is supposed to nourish and purify the blood, to act as a cordial, and to in every way benefit those who are ailing. (Here in America we are more prone to rush to the corner drugstore for our depuratives, nervines, and tonics than to grow them in our gardens!)

Even if Chinese chives are never grown for food or medicine, this species is worthy of a place in every garden. It is one of the most attractive of the *Alliums,* with long, grasslike leaves arching downward at the tips, and erect two-foot-tall flower stalks bearing fragrant, white, starlike flowers rising from this fountain of green.

The plants are easy to grow, and may be started from seed or by division of the rhizomous root. Like the iris, these rhizomes grow in a horizontal fashion, branching out in various directions. On the lower surface of each branch (or division) are large, cordlike roots. When planted, these divisions begin their own cycle of multiplication, eventually growing into a dense clump. To maintain proper nutrition, the clumps should be lifted and divided about every three years.

In the South these plants are evergreen and can be harvested for use at any time. As with common chives, the leaves of this species are cut close to the soil line to encourage the production of new leaves from the cut.

Gardeners in cold climates, where the plants die back during the winter, usually pot a clump of these chives for winter use.

Leaves of this species are used in the same way as common chives; only the flavor is different. They are more strongly flavored and taste like garlic, not onion.

Allium chinense G. Don. There are no groups within the species, but there are several cultivars of Japanese origin. Do not be confused by the similarity of the botanical name of this species *(A. chinense)* and the common name (Chinese chives) of the last species described. Although both are native to China, Japan, and the countries of southeastern Asia, they are entirely different species.

Rakkyo *(A. chinense* G. Don), a perennial onion, is not well known as a cultivated plant in the United States, but almost everyone has eaten it! These are the little pickled onions that we find in specialty food stores. Barrels of them are shipped into our country each year from the Orient, especially Japan.

The truth is, I had never heard of an onion named rakkyo until the day my copy of the *Hortus Third* arrived. That was the day I found a gold mine of research material for this book.

Being an onion lover (and grower) from way back, I had thought I was fairly well informed on the subject of onion species that were used for food. Our herb farm catalog had listed close to a dozen different kinds for years.

What a surprise I had in store when I saw what *Hortus Third* had to offer! This prodigious volume lists some two hundred species of *Alliums,* including not only those that are cultivated for food but those that grow wild within our shores and in other countries as well.

When I came across the name "rakkyo," I just assumed that it was one of the wild ones and thought no more about it. A few weeks later, when I was seeking more detailed cultural information about some of the less-common species, a professor at nearby Texas A&M University suggested that I try to locate a volume titled *Onions and Their Allies* by Henry A. Jones and Louis K. Mann. But it wouldn't be easy, he told me, for the book was now out of print. I finally obtained a copy through an interlibrary loan from another of our state universities.

And there was rakkyo—not an insignificant wild one, as I had thought, but, according to Jones and Mann, one of the world's seven commercially important *Alliums* that are grown for food.

The thing that surprised me most was that out of the dozens of books I had already researched, not one of them except for *Hortus Third* had even mentioned an onion named rakkyo. And I've found no reference to it in volumes I have examined since.

Despite the fact that no other material appears to be available, I would consider my own listing incomplete if I failed to pass on the information about this species that Jones and Mann give:

Allium chinense, known to the Japanese as *"rakkyo"* and to the Chinese as *"ch'iao t'ou,"* is a vegetable onion which is native to central and eastern China and has spread by cultivation to much of eastern Asia. It is grown to a limited extent in California, and probably as a home-garden vegetable by Japanese and Chinese people in many other parts of the world. No botanical varieties of the plant have been described.

Rakkyo, like *A. cepa,* forms conspicuous bulbs. However, because of its small stature and the rapid multiplication of the bulbs to form clumps, the above-ground parts resemble the common chive. The foliage leaves have sheathing bases and hollow blades as in *A. cepa,* but the very slender scape is solid. The bulbs, unlike those of *A. cepa,* consist of foliage leaf-bases only; storage sheaths with aborted blades are not produced. The bulb is formed from the thickened bases of several foliage leaves which appear as concentric rings in the cross-section of the bulb. (pp. 44, 60)

Rakkyo has one feature that sets it apart from all other cultivated *Alliums:* it has both hollow leaves *and* a solid flower stem. All other species that have hollow leaves—the common onion, Welsh onion, and chives—have hollow stems. And the species with solid stems—garlic, leek, and Chinese chives—have flat leaves.

Another characteristic that sets rakkyo apart is the time of year when its somewhat nodding, purple flowers appear. Whereas most *Alliums* produce their blossoms in the spring before the bulbs become dormant, rakkyo waits until fall, when the dormant period has passed.

This plant is propagated by bulb division only; the flowers do not set seed. In our country bulbs are planted in early spring or fall, spaced eight or nine inches apart. By midsummer, when the leaves die back and the period of dormancy begins, each bulb will have produced a nestlike cluster of perhaps a dozen or more bulbs, which are held together by a common stem at their base.

Following the rest period, flower stems and new leaves emerge, both at the same time. The flower stalks rise from the center of old leaves; the new leaves come from offsets that have formed.

Like the common onion, rakkyo's outer scales are thin and dry, but their color is always white or gray. And, like all members of the onion tribe, rakkyo has long been esteemed for its curative powers. It is said to have been used as a drug in China as long ago as three thousand years.

Allium sativum L. There are no groups within the species. However, there are two forms of *A. sativum:* the one we know as **common garlic** and a less-familiar form called rocambole or serpent garlic.

As mentioned earlier, there is an ancient legend that when Satan stepped out from the Garden of Eden after the fall of man, garlic sprang up from the spot where he placed his left foot, and onion from the place where his right foot touched. We have no way of proving or disproving old legends, but we can be sure that garlic (*A. sativum* var. *sativum* L.) has been grown and relished as a food since antiquity; its culture and use are noted in our earliest records.

One such report is found in Beatrice Bliss' reedition of *Chinese Medicinal Herbs*, said to be the greatest and most complete medical treatise ever published in China: "Garlic has been known to the Chinese from a very early period; it being mentioned in the *Calendar of the Hsia*, a book of two thousand years before Christ" (p. 27). A more familiar record comes from the Bible. In the story of Moses leading the Israelites out of bondage and through the wilderness in search of the Promised Land, the children of Israel, forgetting the hardships they had known in Egypt, remembered only the good things they had left behind and complained bitterly to Moses: "We remember the fish which we did eat in Egypt freely . . . and the onions and the garlic" (Num. 11:5).

In those days, according to Pliny, garlic was ranked among the gods; it was literally worshiped by the Egyptians and was sworn to at the taking of an oath. It was regarded as indispensable, not only as a food and a condiment, but as a medicine as well.

In his *Notes on Edible Plants*, Sturtevant tells us that the Roman rulers are said to have disliked garlic on account of the strong scent but fed it to their laborers to strengthen them and to their soldiers to excite courage.

Present-day reports show that garlic is consumed at the rate of thirty-five million pounds a year, second only to the common onion as the most extensively used member of the cultivated *Alliums*. Yet at the same time, no other herb or condiment in history has ever been regarded with such disdain and disgust. It is one of the seasonings that seems to have no middle ground; you either relish it, or you detest it.

Whether you relish it or not, if you're serious about organic gardening you'll be wise to include a clove of garlic here and there among your plantings. It won't take up much room and won't cost much, but the dividends will be well worth the space, time, and money spent.

All *Alliums* are famous for keeping enemy insects at bay, and garlic, with its strong, pungent odor, is the leader of the band. As a growing plant, the odor is not noticable to humans unless it is crushed, but insects apparently find it undesirable in any form. It is the one repellent plant that seems to be offensive to just about every enemy insect you will find in your orchard or garden.

When used as a spray, garlic helps to purge the garden and orchard not only of insects but of certain plant diseases as well. In *Organic Plant Protection*, by Roger B. Yepson, Jr., reports the results of various experiments on the use of garlic spray as an insecticide and as an antibiotic for controlling plant diseases: "Researchers at the University of California found that garlic sprays effectively controlled downy mildew of cucumber and radish, cucumber scab, bean rust, bean anthracnose, early blight of tomato, brown rot of stone fruits, angular leaf spot of cucumber, and bacterial blight of beans" (p. 114).

A recipe for making the garlic spray is also included in the text:

> Take three ounces of chopped garlic bulbs and let it soak in about two teaspoons of mineral oil for 24 hours. Then slowly add a pint of water in which ¼ ounce of pure (not detergent) soap has been dissolved, and stir well. Strain the liquid through fine gauze, and store in a china or glass container, as it reacts with metals. Try the spray against your worst pests, starting with a dilution of 1 part to 20 parts water, and then watering the spray down to 1 part in 100. You'll probably want to use as little garlic as possible if you depend on store-bought cloves, as they're quite expensive.

(Note: Before paying store price, try your local feed and seed store for garlic; it's much cheaper.)

You'll find many variations of this recipe in organic gardening books and magazines. Some growers give their enemies an extra punch by adding hot peppers to the brew. This can be done by including a half dozen ground-up hot pepper pods, or, if fresh peppers are not available, four teaspoons of red pepper powder.

In *Companion Planting for Successful Gardening*, Louise Riotte also suggests adding a teaspoon of fish emulsion as a deterrent to rabbits that may be feasting in your garden. This sounds like an excellent idea; besides keeping the rabbits away, the fish emulsion is also one of the best natural fertilizers.

Requirements for growing garlic are much the same as for growing onions. It is not fussy about the variety of soil it grows in as long as it drains well and is reasonably fertile. There should be enough humus in the soil to retain moisture, and the soil must be loose enough to permit development of the bulbs.

Unlike the common onion, which has hollow leaves and stems, the leaves of garlic are flat and grasslike with a lengthwise fold, and the stems are solid, rising to a height of about two feet and topped with pompomlike clusters of bulbs and flowers mingled together. The flowers are small and white and are lovely for use in dried arrangements, but if it's first-rate bulbs you're trying to grow, you should nip out these flower stems as soon as they begin to form. If they are allowed to develop, the hard seed stalk will leave an undesirable core in the center of the garlic bulb.

Fall is the best time for planting garlic, but it can be planted in winter or very early spring, depending on the area. It is extremely frost-hardy, and even in freezing areas it can be planted in the fall if planted early enough—in September or October—to establish good root growth before severe weather moves in. Growth may be halted during the freezing months, but it will begin again as soon as the snows are gone.

Although the small bulblets in the garlic flower head can be used for propagation, this method is seldom followed. The process is slow; it takes up to two years to produce an average-sized bulb. Garlic is generally propagated by planting the underground cloves singly about an inch deep and four to six inches apart.

The cloves should not be separated until time for planting, as they do not keep as well after separation. I have read that garlic should not be stored under refrigeration, as this causes the bulbs to be nubby and rough. Also, bulbs should not be stored in an overly warm room or sprouting may occur.

Cultivation is required only to control weeds and to break the hard surface crust. Keep cultivation shallow to avoid injury to the small feeding roots. Or, better yet, apply a three-inch mulch as soon as the row is planted. The garlic will grow through the mulch.

As with onions, day length and temperature influence the time when garlic bulbs begin to form, and development is speeded up when temperatures are high. Maturity is indicated when tops die back. The procedure for harvesting, curing, and storing is the same as for onions.

Gerard called **Rocambole** (*A. sativum* var. *ophioscorodon* [Link] Döll) viper's garlic, an early name for serpent garlic. It has had other common names: sand leek, giant garlic, Spanish garlic, all erroneous. It has also been known by various botanical names, starting with the incorrect *A. scorodoprasum* given it by Clusius.

Identification of this perennial has been confusing botanists since 1601, when Clusius listed it in *Rariorum plantarum historia*. Which species should it properly be attributed to? Common garlic? Great-headed garlic? Or, did it belong in an entirely separate classification, a species of its own? Eighteenth-century botanists could not agree.

Botanists Link and Döll contended the plant was of the *A. sativum* group and gave it the variety name *ophioscorodon*. Others insisted the name *A. scorodoprasum*, as listed by Clusius, should stand. And still others believed that the plant did not belong in either of those groups, but should be included in the *A. ampeloprasum* classification.

So much controversy arose during those years that Heinrich Adolph Schrader, a botanist from Hildesheim, Germany, declared a new name for the plant: *Allium controversum*. Eduard August von Regel, another prominent botanist of the day, supported Schrader's stand in regard to the appendage *controversum*, but he insisted the plant was of the *sativum* species, and the plant was again renamed: *Allium sativum* variety *controversum*.

Apparently there were die-hards among botanical writers, for the old name listed by Clusius found its way into many impressive works. And the name *A. sativum* var. *ophioscorodon*, which had been proposed by Link and Döll, kept resurfacing.

The controversy still wasn't over! In 1955, *Baileya*, a quarterly journal published at the Bailey Hortorium of Cornell University, issued a list of valid names of all *Alliums* believed to be in cultivation. Schrader and Regel's name, *A. sativum* var. *controversum*, was included.

Then in 1975 along came *Hortus Third*, the new standard reference to plant names, and the name *"controversum"* was declared obsolete. Rocambole is now known in botanical directories as *A. sativum* var. *ophioscorodon*, the name selected by Döll more than a century ago.

Rocambole resembles common garlic, including the small bulblets in its flower head, but it's a much larger plant, up to three feet in height. The underground bulbs are larger than those of common garlic, and the flavor is milder. The culture and uses of the two species are much the same.

Rocambole has one distinguishing characteristic that is not present in any other member of the onion-garlic family: as maturity approaches and buds begin to form, a long, pointed green cap forms at the top of the flowering scape. The stem rises high above the foliage, then coils about itself, eventually straightening out again and continuing upward. With both stem and head erect, the buds open and the green cap falls to one side, exposing numerous tiny bulblets among the flowers.

These bulblets, usually no larger than a grain of barley, are like miniature garlic bulbs and can be used, fresh or dried, for any purpose where the flavor of garlic is needed. They are particularly useful when only a small amount of garlic flavor is desired. They are used without peeling; the skin needs only to be pierced to allow the flavor to be released.

After flowering, the plant goes into a dormant period until cool weather returns. If underground bulbs are to be harvested, they should be dug when the leaves begin to yellow and the dormant period begins.

If top bulbs are to be saved for seasoning, they are usually dried by hanging the stems upside down. Or they can be dried by standing the stems upright in a tall container, like a bouquet, allowing good air circulation through the flower heads.

Planting time and culture of rocambole is much the same as for common garlic. It is usually propagated by division of the underground bulb. Single cloves are planted about two inches deep and six to eight inches apart.

Plants can be started from the top sets, but it takes at least two years to produce a mature garlic bulb. To avoid a hard center core in the underground bulb, plants should not be allowed to flower.

Allium Ampeloprasum L. Three horticultural groups are recognized in this classification: the *Ampeloprasum* Group, the *Porrum* Group, and the *Kurrat* Group.

Today **great-headed garlic** (*A. ampeloprasum*, Ampeloprasum Group) is known as elephant garlic, a misnomer, for the truth is, it isn't really a garlic at all. It is more closely related to the leek.

Gerard likened it to a "degenerate garlic grown monstrous" (p. 181), a most fitting description, for it does resemble garlic, although larger in all its parts. It has greater height, wider leaves, larger flower heads, and extralarge underground bulbs.

In fact, some growers claim to produce bulbs eight times as large as those of common garlic and weighing up to a pound or more each. To accomplish this, the soil must be in excellent condition—deeply tilled, loose and friable, rich in essential nutrients, preferably in the form of composted organic matter that not only will feed the plants but will retain needed moisture in the soil as well.

Great-headed or elephant garlic has several characteristics that distinguish it from common garlic. The most prominent, of course, is the "monstrous" bulb. Common garlic bulbs are usually three inches or fewer in diameter, whereas elephant garlic is usually two or three times bigger around, even with less than the best growing conditions.

It produces two distinct sizes of cloves within the bulb, while those of common garlic are of uniform size. And offset bulbs are produced around the main bulb of elephant garlic, but never around the bulb of common garlic.

Another distinguishing feature is in the flower head. The flower buds of common garlic are white to pinkish in color, and instead of opening into blossoms they develop into bulbils, which may be used fresh or dried for seasoning. The flower heads of elephant garlic are large like those of the leek and more white than pink in color, and they do not produce the bulbils.

In place of several large cloves within the bulb, elephant garlic frequently produces what is known as a round—a single, large, onionlike bulb without clove segments. This happens because the plants have a tendency to bloom only every other year, and bulbs do not separate into cloves until it is time for the plant to flower. When these "rounds" are produced, they are usually saved for replanting. They will divide into cloves the next year.

As with rocambole and common garlic, the bulbs of elephant garlic should not be divided until time for planting. Cloves are set one to two inches below the surface (depending on their size), and they are spaced eight to ten inches apart in the row.

Elephant garlic's cloves are larger and also more rounded than those of common garlic, and they are milder in taste, with a flavor that is intermediate between common garlic and leek.

Leeks (*A. ampeloprasum* L., Porrum Group) are usually started from seeds like onions. They may be sown directly in the garden or started in a specially prepared bed and transplanted.

The usual practice is to set the plants four to six inches apart in trenches and gradually draw the soil around them as they grow. Trenching is not necessary to produce tender stalks; its purpose is to produce thicker and longer stalks. Under favorable conditions, these stalks often grow up to two or three inches in diameter and ten to fifteen inches long, depending on the depth of the trench.

Surface planting will also produce long, thick stems if the soil is hilled up against the plants as they develop.

Leeks aren't usually classified as multipliers, because they are commonly grown as an annual crop and are harvested at maturity like onions. But they will multiply if they are allowed to remain in place.

When plants are grown as an annual crop, harvesting should take place before the flower heads form, as this causes the stems to toughen and take on a strong, pungent flavor.

In the North, leeks are usually planted very early in the spring for a late summer harvest. Successive later plantings supply leeks throughout the summer, winter, and early spring. In the South, they are planted in spring or fall.

Leeks are hardy, and even in an extremely cold climate they can be harvested through the winter if the plants are covered with a mulch to keep the ground from freezing.

As with many members of the onion tribe, there are several varieties (cultivars) of leeks: Giant Musselberg, Lyon, Broad London, more commonly known in the United States as Large American Flag, and undoubtedly the most popular among home gardeners.

The perennial **perpetual leek**, also known as multiplying leek, comes to us from southern Europe. It is my favorite, and a favorite with Yankee Peddler Herb Farm customers. You plant it once, and you have it growing forever.

Like the common leek, it is a handsome plant, up to thirty inches high during bloom, thickly foliaged at the base, with wide, flat, folded leaves growing in a V formation up the thickish stem. Flowers, which appear in spring, are pinkish white in dense umbels, and though seeds are plentiful, we never found it necessary to use that method for propagation.

Cloves or bulblets, up to an inch or more in diameter, multiply freely around the "mother" plant and send up green shoots, which quickly form into a clump.

These sweet, mild-flavored scallions are as tasty as any green onion that grows, and can be harvested any time of the year by pulling them one at a time or as many as are needed. As with the common leek, the flavor is not as delicate after the plant has flowered.

We propagated this plant by division, either lifting the whole clump and resetting divisions, or by pulling only the side shoots for planting.

When a clump is lifted, there are always a number of small bulblets around the base of the main plant. These too will develop into plants if covered with soil.

Besides perpetual leek's use as scallions, the small bulbs that form at the base of the plant are used as pickling onions, or are chopped into soups, salads, and stews.

Like the leek, to which it is closely related, the **kurrat** (*A. ampeloprasum* L., Kurrat Group) and its culture and uses can be traced back thousands of years. This member of the onion family is not well known in the United States, but it has long been cultivated for food in other parts of the world, particularly in Egypt, its native country.

The leek and the kurrat are so alike in appearance that early botanists considered them to be one and the same. Then in 1925, according to Jones and Mann in *Onions and Their Allies*, kurrat was finally given its own botanical name, *Allium kurrat* Schweinfurth ex Krause. With the publication of *Hortus Third*, the species became known simply as *A. ampeloprasum* L., Kurrat Group.

In appearance, leek and kurrat vary only in size. Kurrat plants are much smaller than leeks, and the leaves are not as wide.

Leeks are grown for their long, white, tender stems and kurrats are grown for their green tops, which are eaten fresh or used as seasoning. Both species are started from seed.

WILD ONIONS

Of the hundreds of members of the *Allium* family, only seven (and their related forms) are commonly cultivated for food. However, this does not rule out the edibleness of the others.

Wild onions were regular fare in the diet of the Indians and early settlers, and were used in folk medicine as well. Yet for some unaccountable reason, many persons who recognize and admire such resourcefulness in the lives of early Americans consider these mavericks of the onion tribe to be unsafe, perhaps even poisonous.

According to the late Euell Gibbons, who spent years gathering wild foods as a hobby, all wild onions are edible. In *Stalking the Wild Asparagus*, he says: "There are no poisonous species of wild onion and all may be used for food, although some kinds are much better flavored than others." Perhaps this "better flavor" (p. 102) is the reason he names only a few: wild garlic, wild leek, and the wild nodding onion. All are native to our country, and he recommends them for use in cooking and pickling. You'll have no trouble identifying them, the experts tell us. They all grow from a basal bulb, have tubular or flat leaves, and a characteristic onion odor.

The field garlic *(A. vineale)* Gibbons mentions is not a native; it came to us from Sweden, nor was it one of his favorites. It isn't harmful to eat, he says, but it has a very strong and penetrating taste and odor that make it undesirable. However, he does approve of using the tender young leaves gathered in spring for chopping into salads.

Wild garlic *(A. canadense)* was one of his favorites. It is found in meadows and open woods throughout eastern North America, from New Brunswick to Florida, and west to the Plains. Wild garlic makes its appearance early in spring and grows about a foot high, producing both underground bulbs and small clusters of top bulbs as well.

The underground bulbs are scallionlike in form, and though they often grow in clusters, they do not have a common membranous covering like those of the garden variety. Nor are the flower heads as large as those of ordinary garlic, but they are the same pinkish white and also produce tiny clovelike bulblets in the inflorescence.

All parts of the plant are edible. For use in pickling, the clusters of top bulbs are harvested before they are completely ripe and used whole. When just a little garlic flavor is desired, the top bulblets can be used singly. Either pierce them with the tip of a knife to release the flavor or crush them before adding. The name "garlic" for this plant is something of a misnomer; the flavor is more like that of onion.

Wild leek *(A. tricocccum)* seems to be the universal favorite of all the mavericks of the onion tribe. Its natural range is from New Brunswick to North Carolina, and west to Minnesota and Iowa; however, there are reports of its growing as far south as Tennessee and Georgia.

Because it is a shade lover, it is found in thick woods, ravines, and coves. The plants often grow in colonies, producing clusters of thick, cylindrical bulbs up to two inches long. Leaves of this species are large and flat—like those of the lily of the valley—about two or three inches in width and five or more inches long.

Whereas most onions flower while the leaves are still green, this wildling waits until the foliage has died back, then sends up a slender, leafless stalk with umbrellalike clusters of creamy white flowers. To be assured of a harvest, the bulbs must be dug before the flowers also disappear. After flowering, in June or July, the plants become dormant and will not show themselves until spring comes again.

Ramp is the name by which this species is known in many regions. In the southern Appalachian Mountains, where it signals the arrival of spring, ramp hunting is an annual community affair, and festivals are held to celebrate the harvest.

The foliage and bulbs are used in salads and soups; the juice of freshly crushed bulbs is said to be useful in treating insect stings.

Sturtevant, in *Notes on Edible Plants,* lists twenty-five *Alliums* that are used for food, many of which grow wild within our shores, and several that are cultivated as ornamentals in flowerbeds, rock gardens, and the like. Nodding onion, prairie onion, and the red-flowered and purple-flowered onions are just a few of our natives that are both edible and ornamental.

Nodding onion *(A. cernuum)* is the prettiest of all the mavericks, and worthy of a place in any perennial border. It is listed in so many gardening books that most gardeners never think of it as anything but ornamental. Flowers begin to appear in June and continue throughout the summer as loose, pendulous clusters of bell-shaped, rose-colored blossoms nodding above long, narrow, grasslike leaves.

It's a low-growing plant, eight to twenty inches high, and is found on rocky slopes and hillsides from New York to South Carolina, and west to British Columbia and California. The bulbs are cylindrical, and not more than half an inch in diameter, but the strong flavor they impart in cooking makes up for their diminutive size. As with many of the wild onions, parboiling improves their flavor.

Prairie onion *(A. stellatum)* is a late bloomer. It flaunts globular clusters of lilac pink long after blossoms of other *Alliums* have faded. The narrow, flat leaves usually wither and disappear before the flowers open. Flowering continues in most areas through October, after which the plant becomes dormant.

This native is found on rocky slopes and prairies from western Illinois and Minnesota, west to Nebraska and Kansas, and as far south as northeastern Texas.

Red-flowered onion *(A. acuminatum)* is another beauty that is often found in ornamental gardens. Flowering time begins in May and lasts through September. The deep rose-purple heads fade to a lighter tint as the season advances.

This species likes a dry environment and grows among brush and pines on the western mountain slopes, foothills, and plains of Colorado, Arizona, and northern California.

Leaves are short and very narrow and grow near the base of the plant, with stalks rising a foot to eighteen inches above them. When seen from a distance, the flowers appear as a purple mist and hold their color long after the earth around them has become barren.

Purple-flowered onion *(A. brevistylum)*, also a mountain dweller, flourishes in woods and meadows at altitudes of eight thousand to ten thousand feet. Its native range is from Montana south to Utah and Colorado.

It's a leafy plant, with flat, narrow, linear blades. Bulbs are slender and appear at the end of a stout rhizome. At maturity they send up scapes one to two feet high, topped with umbels of dark rose flowers.

Bulbs of these ornamental or wild onions do not develop into fat, meaty globes like those of the common onion. But what they lose in size they make up for in pungency and availability. Every state can boast of at least one of these mavericks. There are said to be some fifty varieties in the Rocky Mountain region alone.

"The nose knows when it has found a member of the Onion tribe" (p. 157), writes Euell Gibbons in *Stalking the Wild Asparagus.* But does it always? What about other species of plants that have an onion odor: desert lily *(Hesperocallis undulata),* blue fennel lily *(Androstephium coeruleum),* spring star flower *(Ipheion uniflorum),* and society garlic *(Tulbaghia violacea)*? Are these edible just because they smell like onions?

Of these four species, only desert lily is listed in Sturtevant's *Edible Plants of the World.* Richard Spellenberg, author of *The Audubon Society Field Guide to North American Wildflowers (Western Region)* also tells us that "the bulbs of this species, the only one in its genus, were once used by Indians for food" (p. 583).

After hours of research, I still have been unable to turn up any

73

evidence for or against dining on the onion-scented spring star flower, society garlic, or blue fennel lily, so I'm playing it safe by staying with the varieties that I *know* are edible.

While it's true that only a few nonedible plants have the characteristic onion odor, there are many plants with onionlike foliage that grow from a basal bulb, and some of these are poisonous.

Star-of-Bethlehem *(Ornithogalum umbellatum)* and narcissus species—narcissus, daffodil, and jonquil—are examples. Although these beauties are usually regarded as subjects for ornamental gardens, some of the hardy strains of the species have naturalized in the United States and have poisoned both people and cattle.

Deathcamas *(Zigadenus* species) and fly poison *(Amianthium muscitoxicum)*, both wildlings, are other onionlike plants that have taken their toll in lives. Before blooming, either could be mistaken for an *Allium*, except for one thing: even when the foliage is crushed, they do not have the characteristic odor that all onions have.

Fly poison—also known as crow poison—is said to be even more toxic than deathcamas, and reportedly has killed people who have just touched their hands to their mouths after handling the foliage or root of the plant. Both this villain and deathcamas are extremely poisonous. Farm animals are poisoned not only during grazing but also by eating hay containing any part of the plant.

The moral of the story has to be "Know your onions!" Then you won't be fooled by these wolves in sheep's clothing when you go on your foraging trips.

Perhaps you'd prefer to do your "foraging" in the wilds of your own backyard. If so, you will find these mavericks of the onion tribe easy to tame. Search them out when they make their appearance early in the spring. Simply dig up the bulbs, divide them, and replant them in your garden or wherever you want them to grow. Try to select soil and climatic conditions as close as possible to the place where you originally found them growing. They are perennial, and will reward you with wild onions for years to come.

Table 5 lists a few of the mavericks of the onion tribe, along with characteristics that should be helpful in identifying them. All are native to our shores and the ones most commonly foraged for food.

Table 5. Mavericks of the Onion Tribe

Allium Species and Common Names	Color of Flowers	Time of Bloom	Height (inches)	Leaves	Bulbs	Habitat	Natural Range
A. Acumination Hooker's Onion Red-flowered Onion	Deep rose-purple	May–July	12	2 or more 1/8" wide, shorter than scape	Globe-shaped with membranous netted coats	Foothill woods and meadows	British Columbia to northern California, east to Montana, Colorado, and Arizona
A. brevistylum Purple-flowered Onion	Dark rose to purple	Late spring	12–24	Several, linear leaves flat to 1/4" wide, near base of plant	Slender fibrous-coated bulbs at end of stout rhizome	Montane woods and meadows (8,000–10,000 ft.)	Montana, Colorado, and Utah
A. breweri Violet-flowered Onion	Deep rose-purple	May–July	3	2 sickle-shaped leaves, much longer than scape	Bulbs not on a rhizome, outer coat membranous, not patterned	Open, often rocky slopes, among brush and pines	Central California

Table 5. Mavericks of the Onion Tribe, continued

Allium Species and Common Names	Color of Flowers	Time of Bloom	Height (inches)	Leaves	Bulbs	Habitat	Natural Range
A. canadense Wild Garlic, Meadow Garlic, Tree Onion, Meadow Onion, Rose Leek, Wild Shallot, Meadow Leek	Pinkish-white flowers, followed by bulbils	May–July	12–24	Usually 3 or more, narrow, grass-like, linear, flat to 18" long	Solitary bulbs with fibrous net-ted coats. Often found in bunches, growing close together	Low meadows and open woods	New Brunswick to Florida, west to the Plains
A. cernuum Nodding Onion, Lady's Leek	Rose or white bell-shaped flowers in nodding clusters	June–Oct.	12–24	Several linear, flat leaves, 4–16" long, clustered at base	Narrow, oblong, thin-coated bulbs, growing in clusters	Rocky slopes and dry hillsides	New York to South Carolina, west to British Columbia and California
A. Coryi Yellow-flowered Onion	Chrome yellow, sometimes red-tinged	April–May	12	2 or 3 very narrow leaves, shorter than scape	Outer bulb coat a fibrous network of open meshes	Plains and hills	Found only in West Texas

Species	Color	Bloom	No.	Leaves	Bulb	Habitat	Range
A. Cuthberti Striped Garlic	White	Mar.–May	20	3 or more narrow leaves, shorter than scape	Bulbs not on a rhizome, outer bulb coat a fibrous network of open meshes	Plains	Coastal plain, North Carolina to Florida and Alabama
A. Douglasii Douglas Onion	Pink or (rarely) white	May–June	10	2 leaves, 1/4" wide, shorter than scape	Bulbs not on a rhizome, outer bulb coat membranous, not patterned	Foothills and meadows	Washington, Oregon and Idaho
A. Drummondii Prairie Onion Sand Onion	White through pink to red, occasionally greenish yellow	Mar.–May	8–12	3 or more leaves, 1/8" wide or wider, about as tall as scape	Bulbs not on a rhizome, outer bulb coat a fibrous network of fine meshes with a membrane	Plains and hills	Texas to New Mexico, south to Mexico, north to western Nebraska
A. Geyeri Wild Onion	Rose-pink	June–Aug.	20	Usually 3 or more narrow leaves, shorter than scape	Bulbs not on a rhizome, outer bulb coat netted	Meadows and moist soils of mountains	Western Texas and southeast Arizona, north to South Dakota and Alberta

Table 5. Mavericks of the Onion Tribe, continued

Allium Species and Common Names	Color of Flowers	Time of Bloom	Height (inches)	Leaves	Bulbs	Habitat	Natural Range
A. haematochiton Red-skinned Onion	Rose to deep purple	May–June	18	Several linear flat leaves, very narrow, about as long as scape	Long slender bulbs with reddish purple membranous coat	Dry hillsides	Southern California to Baja California
A. macropetalum Desert Onion	Pink with reddish midribs	Mar.–May	6–16	2 leaves to 1/8" wide, longer than scape	Bulbs egg-shaped, often clustered, bulb coat fibrous network of open meshes	Desert plains and hills	Colorado to Arizona and West Texas
A. perdulce Sand Onion	Deep rose	Mar.–May	8	3 or more leaves, 1/8" wide, taller than flower stem	Bulbs egg-shaped, often clustered but not on a rhizome, bulb coat netted	Sandy soil, rocky places	Southeast South Dakota and Iowa, south to north central Texas and eastern New Mexico

Species / Common Name	Color	Bloom	No.	Leaves	Bulbs	Habitat	Range
A. rubrum Top Onion	Pink or white umbels with bulbils and few or no flowers	June–Aug.	12	Few leaves, 1/4" or less, shorter than scape	Bulbs not on a rhizome, outer coat fibrous network of open meshes	Montane woods and meadows	New Mexico and Arizona to British Columbia and Alberta
A. Schoenoprasum var. sibiricum Wild Purple Onion Wild Siberian Chive	Rose to rose-violet	July–Aug.	10–24	Several narrow leaves, 8–16" long	Bulbs clustered on a small rhizome, outer bulb coat membranous	Moist soils of woods and meadows	Throughout northern North America
A. stellatum Autumn Wild Onion Prairie Onion	Lavender-pink	July–Oct.	18	Several leaves which usually disappear before flowers open	Elongate bulbs, outer bulb coat membranous	Rocky slopes and prairies	Western Illinois and Minnesota, west to Nebraska and Kansas
A. textile Textile Onion	Varies from white to deep pink, with reddish brown midveins	May–June	12	Usually 2 leaves, very narrow, shorter than scape	Solitary underground bulbs, covered with fibrous netted coats	Open woods and prairies	Minnesota and Manitoba to Alberta, south to Colorado, New Mexico, and Utah

Table 5. Mavericks of the Onion Tribe, continued

Allium Species and Common Names	Color of Flowers	Time of Bloom	Height (inches)	Leaves	Bulbs	Habitat	Natural Range
A. tricoccum Ramp	Large creamy-white clusters	June–July	6–20	2 or 3 flat, lance-head-shaped leaves, 1–3" wide, up to 8" or 9" long	Bulbs largest of the wild onions, elongate in shape, growing singly or on a rhizome	Rich woods, ravines, and coves	New Brunswick to Minnesota, south to North Carolina and Iowa
A. validum Swamp Onion	Rose to nearly white	June–Oct.	18–30	Several narrow, linear leaves, nearly as long as scape	Slender bulbs, growing at the tip of a stout rhizome, membranous coats	High mountain regions	Washington to California, east to western Nevada

NOTE: Common names may vary from region to region. Time of bloom, even height and color may vary in different locales.

4

Insects That Pester Onions

THRIPS

With the fine reputation the onion family has for protecting other garden plants against insect invasion, you would think they'd be immune to any such problems of their own.

Not so. Although some varieties—Welsh onion, Egyptian onion, and other multiplying types—are less vulnerable to attack, the common onion is susceptible to a number of potential hazards capable of destroying the storage crop.

Thrips *(Thrips tobaci)*, a minute, spindle-shaped, flying insect, is enemy number one in the onion patch and is said to cause more damage than all other insects and diseases combined. They multiply prolifically, with ten or more generations appearing in a gardening year. The female can reproduce without mating, and both the larvae and the adults cause injury.

Thrips are most common in warm weather, especially in dry seasons. They are usually a pest of young seedlings, but may attack plants at any stage. The female lays her eggs in the tender, inner leaves of the plant, where the young will be protected from the elements and insect predators. The eggs hatch in two to ten days, depending on the temperature, and the emerging larvae immediately begin to feed on the tender leafpoints. The larvae pass through two molting stages while feeding on the plants and complete their growth in about five days. Then they enter the soil to pupate and emerge as adults four days later. Thus a generation is completed in about two weeks. Generations overlap considerably, with all stages possibly being in the garden at the same time during the season.

Thrips feed by puncturing the surface of the leaves and sucking out the juices. The damage first appears as dashes, where the leaf or stem has been pierced, then these dashes streak together in whitish blotches. Severely attacked plants develop a gray or silvery appearance and may become distorted and die.

Adult thrips average about $\frac{1}{25}$-inch long, are usually light brown in color, and may be found in great numbers on the underside of leaves of affected plants. The larvae, which are white or very pale yellow, resemble adults but are smaller and have no wings. Adult males are also wingless.

In the South, onion thrips feed on onions and other host plants throughout the winter. In the North, they pass the winter on onion plants left in the gardens and in the crowns of other host plants, such as alfalfa and clover. They also winter in discarded onions, and sometimes in stored bulbs.

One way of preventing their survival through the winter is to clean up all refuse that harbors them. Till in or bury old onion trimmings and other garden residue; cut and burn grass and tall weeds in waste places where they hibernate.

During the gardening season, driving rains or a thorough spraying with the hose may wash thrips from the plants and destroy them, and ladybugs and syrphid flies may help to keep them in check.

The syrphid fly should not be confused with the onion fly, which is responsible for the onion maggot. The onion fly resembles a housefly except that it is only about half the housefly's size, and its body is a light greenish gray. Syrphid flies usually are brightly colored. Some have bright yellow-and-black-banded bodies and buzz loudly, so they are often mistaken for bees. The females lay their eggs on leaves and shoots of plants infested with thrips, and the newly hatched larvae capture and destroy the pests but are harmless to the plants.

Breeding for resistance to thrips has been under way for some time, but total control still seems a long way off. Onion thrips occur wherever onions grow, making them a problem for growers throughout the United States.

ONION MAGGOTS

Onion maggots *(Hylemya antiqua)* are not as widely distributed as thrips, and their attacks are sporadic, with damage varying from year to year. This grub feeds on onion plants of all ages, from the youngest seedlings to mature bulbs.

Onion maggots are the larvae of the onion fly, a long-legged, large-winged, bristly-bodied insect that resembles the housefly, except that it is only about half the size and its body is a light greenish gray. Onion flies are quite noticeable as they fly over the plants and run about the ground where onions are growing.

The female lays her eggs—usually thirty or forty at a time—in the leaf axils or in the crevices in the soil near the plant. Later in the season, when onions are nearing maturity and protrude above the ground, the eggs may be deposited directly on the bulbs. These white eggs hatch in two to seven days, depending on the temperature, and the small, legless maggots emerge to crawl down the plant and into the bulb. There they feed for two or three weeks before entering the pupal stage.

Pupation occurs in the soil near the plant and lasts for another two or three weeks, after which another swarm of onion flies emerges to repeat the cycle.

Onion plants known to be infested with maggots should be pulled and burned as soon as the maggots are observed, and the soil where the onions grew should be examined carefully for maggots or puparia that may have been left behind.

The full-grown maggot is white, up to one third-inch long, and resembles the housefly maggot. The puparia varies in color from light yellowish brown to a dark reddish brown.

Several broods of these grubs are produced during the season. The last brood winters in the pupal stage. They also hibernate in the shelter of weeds and crop residue and emerge with the first warm breath of spring.

In northern gardens, where onion maggots are most common, damage can be quite extensive, especially in the spring and early summer, when plants are young. If infestation is bad, an entire crop may be lost as the maggots move along the rows, boring through the bulbs, spreading disease, and destroying the underground parts. Seedlings usually die, and mature bulbs are damaged beyond use. Infestation is indicated by yellowing foliage, which later turns white and falls.

One way to outwit this pest is to spot-plant onions throughout the garden, instead of in a row. Since the maggots travel from plant to plant seeking nourishment, it isn't be so easy for them to find their next meal. They also feed on all sorts of decaying plants, so good garden practice should be followed. Large amounts of decaying organic matter should not be used in soils where maggots are a problem.

Old-timers used wood ashes as a method of control, sprinkling the soil around the plants when they were two or three inches high. This practice is still popular with many gardeners.

Tar paper collars covering the soil around the plants are also effective in discouraging the onion fly, but this method is almost impossible in a large onion patch. The collars are cut from felt roofing paper, which is heavily scented with tar. The scent repels the fly, and she does not light to deposit her eggs.

All onions are susceptible to damage from these maggots, but the Welsh onion shows the greatest resistance.

SEED CORN MAGGOTS

Seed corn maggots *(Hylemya cilicrura)* are closely related to onion maggots, but they are not as common in the onion patch as they are among beans, corn, peas, and potatoes. Where they do occur, however, the damage is severe.

Unlike the onion maggot, which attacks the plant at any stage, the seed corn maggot attacks only the germinating seed and very young seedlings.

The full-grown maggots are yellowish white, about one-quarter inch long, and have sharply pointed heads with which they burrow into the seed, destroying the germ so that no plants are produced. They also carry various bacterial diseases that infect the young seedlings and cause them to die.

Their reproduction process and life cycle is similar to that of the onion maggot. Control measures are the same. The fly responsible for these grubs is grayish brown in color.

Sanitation in the garden is very important. Partly decayed vegetable matter that is left lying about the garden attracts the flies, and soils containing such material are likely to become infested with the maggots. The solution is to plant seed shallow in such areas, and prepare the seedbed to promote germination as rapidly as possible.

CUTWORMS

Cutworms are probably the sneakiest pests in the garden. They spend their days hiding under rocks and trash or buried in the soil, then come out at night to do their dirty work when the gardener isn't around.

There are several different kinds of cutworms, most of them soft-bodied, smooth, plump, cylindrical in shape, and up to an inch and a half long. They vary in color from a greasy gray to brown, some marked with lighter or darker spots or stripes, others so dark brown they appear almost to be black. Whichever the species, they all have one thing in common—voracious appetites!

Cutworms are damaging to almost any kind of tender plant, including onions. When young plants are set out, cutworms cut them off just above the soil surface at night and drag them back to their nearby burrows for feeding. These culprits usually are found by digging into the surface soil around the freshly cut plants.

If you do unearth the thief, squash it, chop it, or beat it to death with a straw if you have to, for each of these grubs has the potential of creating thousands more!

Cutworms are the larval stage of dull-colored night-flying moths, and each female moth may lay up to fifteen hundred eggs! And each female of that brood may lay another fifteen hundred, and each female of that brood . . . and so on and so on. There are four or more generations yearly, depending on the species.

Eggs are usually deposited in grassy or weedy areas, but may be laid directly in the garden if old stalks are left standing. When temperatures are warm, the eggs hatch in a couple of weeks, and the young cutworms immediately begin to feed.

The larval stage lasts for several months, with some species feeding right through the winter. When mature, the caterpillars burrow into the soil and change through the pupal stage into adult moths.

The pupa usually is brown, rather firm-shelled and capsulelike, about one-half to three-fourths inch long, and is easily visible when unearthed. If you find one, step on it, for in a few months it too may be laying fifteen hundred eggs!

Control of cutworms can be maintained by using poison bait. Scatter it around the plants in the evening when the cutworms come out to feed. The bait is prepared by mixing one-half pound sodium fluosilicate *or* Paris green with fourteen pounds of wheat bran and moistening the mixture with water—one-half gallon is about right to form a moist but not overly wet mixture for spreading.

Ecology-minded gardeners and pet owners shy away from this method because this mixture kills dogs, cats, birds, chickens—anything that eats it. But there are less drastic ways to foil the cutworm.

Old-timers used a bait-and-trap-method, one that is still effective in gardens today. Compact handfuls of almost any kind of green vegetation—clover, milkweed, mullein, or vegetables leaves—were spotted about the garden and pressed down with the foot to lure the cutworms to the surface where they could be seen and killed.

Grapefruit and cantaloupe halves, orange rinds, and traps were also used. The bait was placed beneath the trap's boards, then the worms were collected each morning.

Gardeners who aren't afraid of the dark and who are not squeamish about picking up the worms can make a pretty good catch by strolling through the garden with a flashlight at night. Cutworms are easily spotted and are always too fat and clumsy to get away.

The most permanent way of getting rid of cutworms is to starve them out. This is another method relied on by old-timers and still practiced today. The ground is kept tilled of all vegetation when not in use. This cuts off the worms' food supply, and it also disposes of weeds and stalks of other plants where the moth might deposit her eggs.

If new sod is to be broken for a garden, it should be tilled months in advance if possible and kept tilled until time for planting. Grassy areas and sod lands are favorite haunts for both the moth and her young, places for her to deposit her eggs and for the young caterpillars to eat and eat and eat.

WIREWORMS

Wireworms are soil- and root-infesting pests that will attack any field or garden crop. They are especially damaging to onions and other root crops that are planted in newly broken sod.

They injure crops by destroying seeds, cutting off small underground stems, boring holes in larger stems, and tunneling through roots, bulbs, and tubers. What they don't destroy completely, they disfigure so badly that the produce is unfit for use.

They are particularly damaging to onions, potatoes, sweet potatoes, carrots, beets, turnips, beans, lettuce, and melons.

These hard, shiny, six-legged, wirelike worms are usually yellow or brown and have a life cycle of two to six years, depending on the species. The one most damaging to onions is the larva of click beetles (*Limonius* spp.). The adult beetles are usually hardshelled, brownish gray or sometimes nearly black bugs, with long, slender, winged bodies. There are about 350 species of wireworms in the United States and Canada alone.

The click beetle and a valued predatory insect, the ground beetle, are often mistaken for each other when found running about the garden. And many gardeners who think the only good bug is a dead bug stomps on them both!

Both the ground beetle and its grubs, which are often mistaken for wireworms, have sharp, caliperlike jaws that spell death for a number of garden pests: insects, young slugs, snails, mites, caterpillars. One species, the European *Calosoma sycophanta* ground beetle, was valued so highly as a predatory insect that it was actually imported and carefully cultivated in this country to destroy the larvae of gypsy and browntail moths, a measure that proved most effective.

Those who are unfortunate enough to find a click beetle in their garden—and who isn't?—should take time to examine it closely in order to make sure it isn't the friendly ground beetle. The click beetle's body is streamlined and tapered at each end, whereas the ground beetle's body is more rounded, its head more prominent, and its legs longer. The ground beetle always seems to be in a hurry, scurrying about in search of food and ridding the garden of enemies.

Another way to recognize the harmful click beetle, or skipjack as it is sometimes called, is to listen for its "click." When touched or alarmed, the click beetle falls to the ground, folds up its legs, and plays dead. If it's lying on its back, it will throw itself into the air with a sudden jerking motion accompanied by a clicking sound, land on its feet, and scurry away.

Parent click beetles deposit tiny white eggs in the soil in early spring, and the young wireworms emerge within a few days or weeks. After two to six years of feeding, depending on the species, the worms are from one-half to one and a half inches long. They change to pupae during midsummer.

Pupation is usually completed in a few weeks, but the new beetles remain in the soil in earthen cells until spring, when they emerge to lay eggs.

Various insecticides and fumigants are available for treating wireworm-infested areas, but some of these remain in the soil for years and are so deadly to other forms of life that many gardeners are reluctant to use them.

The old-timers used the same bait-and-trap method for wireworms as for cutworms: compact handfuls of green vegetation—clover, milkweed, mullein, elder sprouts, or vegetable leaves from the garden—were spotted about the planted area and pressed down with the foot to lure wireworms to the surface, where they could be collected and killed.

Board traps were also used. Small bunches of green vegetation poisoned with Paris green mixed in water were spotted about the garden and covered with boards to protect household pets, birds, and other wildlife from getting to the poison.

Using this poisoned bait method dispensed with the need for collecting the worms each morning. Large numbers of the parent beetles were also killed this way, as well as other garden pests, slugs, snails, squash bugs, and pill bugs.

All of this sounds like a pretty good idea until you realize that with the poisoned bait many beneficial insects—ground beetles, ladybugs, doodlebugs or ant lions, syrphid flies, wasps, and others—will be exterminated too.

Copperas and saltpeter were said to be effective in ridding the soil of wireworms and were used with crops such as corn. The seed corn was soaked in a solution of copperas and saltpeter—one-fourth pound of each to a bushel of ears of corn. After measuring out the bushel, the corn was shelled, and the copperas and saltpeter were mixed with enough water to cover. The shelled corn was soaked for twelve hours before planting. Not only the wireworms disappeared, but cutworms as well.

Soot, scattered in the drills at planting time, was used for protecting root crops, especially potatoes, from wireworm infestation. After the sets were placed in the drill, the soot was scattered over them, then covered with soil in the usual way.

Wood ashes, with their high potash content were also relied on for foiling wireworms. Besides protecting the onion crop, the potash also supplied a much-needed nutrient for growing a successful onion crop.

Salt, spread over the ground before plowing at the rate of two barrels per acre, was also regarded as an excellent means of wireworm control. Besides its value as an insect repellent, salt was considered a good fertilizer because it attracted and held moisture in the soil. It was common practice in the old days—especially when planting onions or asparagus—to "sow the ground white with salt" before turning it over in the fall. With this method, old-timers hoped the wireworms would all be gone when planting time came again.

Most modern gardeners are appalled at the thought of adding that much salt to the soil. And, since few of us plant a bushel of corn at one time and soot isn't too plentiful in our age of gas and electric heating, these last three control methods may not be our solution.

Those of us who are even more appalled at the thought of poisoning the land where we grow our food rely on another tried-and-true method that has been used for wireworm control since the early days. We starve them out.

If the soil is tilled regularly when no crops occupy it, the worms can find nothing to feed on. This method starves not only wireworms, cutworms, and other soil-abiding pests and destroys all stages of growth but perennial weeds and other noxious vegetation as well.

WOOLLY WORMS

Salt marsh caterpillars *(Estigmene acrea)* are hairy, wormlike creatures with black-and-yellow-banded bodies about two inches long when fully grown. We called then woolly worms or woolly bears when we were children and pretended they were friendly fur-coated little ladies when we found them humping their way across the yard.

As grown-up gardeners we've learned the damage they can do, and our feelings toward them now are anything but friendly. They have voracious appetites and will eat practically anything that grows—garden crops, field crops, weeds, shrubs—and they seldom dine alone.

A heavy infestation of caterpillars may completely strip the plants in a field within a few days. When that food supply is gone, they move on to greener pastures, usually in large numbers, stripping foliage as they go.

This caterpillar is the larva of moths with black-freckled wings. The female moth is white, with yellowish orange on the underside of her wings and body. The abdomen also has frecklelike markings.

In the spring she deposits masses of small, white, flattish eggs in patches on the undersides of leaves, where the young will be able to feed. In a few days the eggs hatch, and the young caterpillars begin their feast, which will last for a month or two before they move underground for the pupation stage.

Mature caterpillars spend the winter in thin silken cocoons. They enter the pupation stage in early spring and emerge as adult moths in late spring or summer.

They are widely distributed throughout the United States and produce up to four generations a year.

SPIDER MITES

Spider mites (*Tetranychus* spp.) are not really insects but relatives of the true spider. They are so small they can hardly be seen without a magnifying glass. They multiply rapidly, especially in hot, dry weather, and produce up to seventeen generations a year.

Also known as red spiders, these pests attack nearly all kinds of vegetation—field crops, vegetables, flowers, weeds, shrubs, trees. They are almost constantly present on garden crops such as beans, cucumbers, tomatoes, eggplants, and melons during July and August.

Spider mites are damaging during all stages of their growth—larval, nymphal, and adult. On onions they are found mostly on the underside of the leaves.

They feed by piercing the outer coating of the leaf and sucking out its juices. This gives the leaf a bleached appearance around the thickly dotted, whitish feeding punctures.

Plants may become covered with fine, silken webs that the spiders spin as they move from place to place. They migrate by crawling on the ground, but they are also carried by wind and water.

In the South the red spider winters in refuse and on green vegetation, or in protected places such as buds and crowns of perennial flowers and weeds. It attacks the new growth as soon as it starts in spring. In the egg stage, others hibernate on the bark and under the bud scales of trees and shrubs. In the North, chiefly adults winter in the soil.

Driving rains sometimes wash these spider mites from the

plants, and frequent hosing also helps check infestation. Dusting with sulfher is effective, as are sprays made from various garden plants—larkspur, nicotiana, coriander, potato, tomato. Sprays made of the onion itself will send these red spiders scurrying from your onion patch.

LEAF MINERS

Leaf miners are the larvae of insects—moths, flies, sawflies, beetles—that feed on the plant tissue between the upper and lower leaf surfaces of a large number of vegetable crops, flowers, shrubs, and trees.

Leaf miners that attack onions are of the *Liriomza* species—tiny, white, wedge-shaped maggots, the larvae of a very small, black-and-yellow, gnatlike fly.

The adult female fly deposits her eggs by puncturing the leaf tissue and inserting the eggs one at a time inside the opening. The eggs hatch in a few days, and the young maggots begin to feed.

They tunnel between the upper and lower skins of the leaf, feeding as they go and leaving meandering trails of white, which are visible to the eye. When leaf miners are present in large numbers, the leaves appear blotched as the threadlike trails cross and recross. The trails eventually girdle the leaf, causing it to wilt. This foliage loss reduces the yield of the crop.

The maggots feed in the leaf tissues for a couple of weeks, then cut an opening in the outer skin and crawl out of the leaf to enter the soil for the pupation stage. Adult flies emerge in five days to begin the cycle all over again.

The life cycle of this pest is completed within about twenty-three days, with up to twenty generations occurring in a single year.

BULB MITES

Bulb mites *(Rhizoglyphys echinopus)* are not considered major onion pests in the garden, but they may cause serious damage to onions in storage.

The chief target of this insect is bulbs that have already been

Onion bud mites appear in this enlargement of the upper portion of a severely infested flower stem. This pest is so minute it is difficult to see, even with a magnifying glass, so infestations are often overlooked. Courtesy Dessert Seed Co.

damaged by insects, disease, or injuries sustained during cultivation and harvesting. The mites breed rapidly on the injured parts. They often occur in swarms beneath the outer scales and among the inner scales of the bulbs. They destroy the bulb by piercing the tissues and drawing out the juices. After destroying one bulb, they move on to another.

Bulb mites also damage other bulbs and tubers in storage—hyacinths, lilies, narcissus, tulips, dahlias, and potatoes.

NEMATODES

Nematodes, also known as eelworms, are slender, round, thread-like creatures, often too small to be visible to the naked eye. If visible, they look like small, whitish threads, rarely more than one-sixteenth of an inch in length.

They are present in soils everywhere, in wet and dry lands, in clayey as well as sandy soils. They thrive whereever plants grow, from the coldest Arctic regions to the warmest tropics. The richer the plant life, the greater their number. And the more activity around the farm or garden, the more widespread these soil pests become.

People are their own worst enemy when it comes to spreading nematodes in the soil. We carry them about on our footwear, on our tools and machinery; we buy them on bulbs and seeds, and on plants from nurseries; they are sometimes present on packing materials, in hay that we use for mulch, or manure we work into his soil. In fact, nematodes may be present in any material that is moved from one point to another in the growing area. Animals and birds, both domestic and wild, are carriers, and wind and water, especially irrigation water, are significant distributors of nematodes.

Although many different species of nematodes exist, only two, the stem and bulb nematode and the root knot nematode, are commonly damaging to onions.

STEM AND BULB NEMATODES *(DITYLENCHUS DIPSACI)*
Stem and bulb nematodes feed in the leaves and stems when onion plants are very young. They move down into the scales when the bulbs begin to mature.

Onions planted in nematode-infested soil are slow to emerge. When the seedlings do come up, they are deformed, and growth is stunted by the worms tunneling through their cells and sapping their juices. The foliage becomes pale and limp, and leaves begin to turn brown and die.

If plants survive to the stage when bulbs begin to enlarge, the nematodes move down the leaves and stems and begin feeding on the outer scales of the bulb. This causes the underlying scales to become soft and crumbly. The skin takes on a frosty, lacelike texture.

Nematodes continue to thrive in infested bulbs after they are harvested and stored. They drain the juices from the cells until only puffy, lightweight bulbs remain.

If such bulbs are found in your onion bin, they should be sorted out and destroyed, preferably by fire, because nematodes can withstand almost any other treatment.

Research has shown that extreme weather conditions have no adverse effect on nematodes, either in the adult stage or the pre-adult larval forms. When moisture becomes available, they are brought back to active life, and the life cycle continues as though there had been no interruption. According to the *Royal Horticultural Dictionary of Gardening:* "The pre-adult larval forms are capable of remaining in a desiccated state for long periods—3 to 7 or more years—again becoming active when placed in moist conditions" (p. 2023).

ROOT KNOT NEMATODES *(TRICODORUS CHRISTIEI)*
Root knot nematodes, also called stubby root nematodes, stunt growth and cause other malformations of the plant by puncturing the roots and draining off the food supply. Without nourishment, the bulbs cannot develop to normal size.

The roots of affected plants are short and stubby, with an unhealthy yellowish color, and are deformed with various-sized swellings or galls. Badly infested roots sometimes form an abnormally large number of fine rootlets, the tips of which are also covered with reddened galls or lesions.

If you examine the galled tissue carefully, you can see a glistening, white, pear-shaped body. This is the female nematode, and within that body may be three hundred to twelve hundred eggs. Consider the potential, if even half of *these* are female!

Various soil fumigants for nematode control have appeared on the market, but most of them are so poisonous that many gardeners will not use them; they prefer the safer biodynamic methods.

Sprays made from asparagus juice are said to be an effective killer of the root knot nematode. And if the foliage of the stately marigold *(Tagetes minuta)* is prepared in a spray or if the plant is grown in the garden, it can clear the soil of these pests.

5

Diseases of Onions

∾

DOWNY MILDEW, WHITE ROT, AND PURPLE BLOTCH

Onions are popular garden vegetables despite the fact that losses from disease are a constant threat regardless of where they are grown. In the northern United States smut is a problem, in the South it's pink root, while many other diseases affecting onions apparently have no territorial boundries.

Diseases of onions and their causes are divided into four groups: fungus diseases, bacterial diseases, virus diseases, and diseases resulting from adverse weather or other unfavorable conditions.

Fungus diseases are the most common, and the most destructive. They spread rapidly as spores are carried by wind, water, insects, or maybe even the gardener. Once the soil is infected it may remain infected for years.

Fungus is a low form of plant life, without leaves, flowers, or green coloring matter (chlorophyll). Fungi are incapable of manufacturing their own food and live off other plants or animals that are dead or alive.

Although there are said to be more than five thousand known species of fungus, there are only two general classes: the saprophyte fungi, which live on dead or decaying matter, and the parasite fungi, which grow on living plants and animals. It is the parasite fungi that we are concerned with.

A fungus body is composed of delicate threads known as hyphae. When many of these threads are branched together into one system, they are called mycelia. This branched system may form inside the plant or on its surface, depending on the species of the fungus.

Although the different species have different branching habits and structures, the proliferation pattern is the same. Growth takes place at the ends of the individual threads (mycelia), but instead of forming seeds, as is the case with higher plant life, fungi multiply by forming spores. Spores are microscopic bodies that function like seeds. When a spore lands on a plant, and conditions are right, a new fungus body quickly begins to grow.

While many diseases affect onions and their close relatives—garlic, chives, shallots, Welsh onions, and leeks—a few cause greater losses, particularly to onions, than others. To these potential hazards I devote the remainder of this book.

DOWNY MILDEW

Downy mildew, caused by the fungus *Peronospora destructor,* is a disease that breeds in the soil. It is also spread by wind-borne spores of the fungus. It affects onions, Welsh onions, leeks, shallots, garlic, and chives by reducing bulb growth and causing bulb tissue to be spongy and of poor keeping quality.

The disease usually appears in midseason. Plants in low muck areas with faulty drainage and poor air circulation are most susceptible, although crops in any area can be affected in seasons that are unusually cool and rainy.

Symptoms first appear as yellowish spots on the upper half of the leaves and stems. The spots soon develop a furry, bluish gray mildew. Within a day or two the tops begin to weaken and turn yellow.

The higher the humidity, the more rapidly the disease advances. Dry weather will halt it temporarily, but if moist conditions continue, the tops will be weakened to the point at which they die back, although the plant itself is seldom killed.

Sanitation is of utmost importance when dealing with downy mildew or any fungus disease. Crop residues should be cleaned up and buried deeply or, better yet, burned, for the spores will continue to form in old leaves and will remain viable in the soil until the next season.

Bulbs or sets from affected areas should not be used for new crops because the fungus threads may live on in these. The fungus grows down into the scales and winters there. The bulbs or sets thus become a host for a new crop of summer spores.

All onion varieties are susceptible to downy mildew, and the use of chemical sprays and dusts has generally not given satisfactory control. In areas where the disease is most prevalent—New York, Michigan, Louisiana, California, and Oregon—onion rows should run the same direction as the prevailing winds, so that the foliage will dry rapidly after rains, dews, and fogs.

Aside from cleaning up old leaves and residue on which spores can breed and rotation with nonrelated crops—that is, waiting four to five years to replant in the same area—little else can be done to combat downy mildew of onions.

WHITE ROT

White rot, caused by the fungus *Sclerotium cepivorum*, attacks the common onion, Welsh onion, leeks, shallots, and garlic. It begins with a yellowing and dying back of the leaves, starting at the tips and progressing downward.

The roots gradually rot away, a semiwatery decay destroys the bulb scales, and the base of the bulb is covered with a white, fluffy growth (mycelia). Later, this growth forms into hard, black, pinhead-sized sclerotia—resting fungus spores. These spores will enter and further contaminate the soil if allowed to remain. Infected plants should be destroyed as soon as the disease is recognized.

There are no satisfactory control methods for this disease. A long rotation with nonrelated crops is advisable as the fungus remains viable in the soil for years.

PURPLE BLOTCH

Purple blotch, caused by the fungus *Alternaria porri*, is a puzzle in the onion patch. Even plant scientists can't say which climatic conditions favor its development. It appears to be most prevalent in

Purple blotch is responsible for the damage to the foliage of these onions. Plants are most susceptible to the disease as the time of maturity approaches. Losses may occur in the field or after the bulbs are in storage. Photo by A. M. Binkley, courtesy Dessert Seed Co.

warm, humid weather; however, losses also occur after the bulbs are placed in cool, dry storage.

The disease usually attacks when the onions are nearing maturity. Symptoms are grayish, deep lesions with dark centers on the leaves and stems. As the lesions enlarge, the dark centers spread into purplish blotches, which may eventually encircle the entire leaf or stem and kill it.

The fungus usually enters the bulb at the neck area, but infection may begin anywhere on the bulb, as a result of bruises that have occurred during harvesting. The disease causes a semiwatery rot of the bulb scales. The scales gradually darken, then dry up. Usually, only the outer scales are affected, but if infection is severe, the entire bulb may be destroyed.

Onion varieties such as Yellow Globe Danvers, Red Creole,

and Abundance, which have a covering of wax or "bloom" on the foliage, are more resistant than varieties with "glossy" foliage, such as Sweet Spanish, Grano, and Bermuda.

PINK ROOT, NECK ROT, AND BASAL ROT

Some fungus diseases of onions can be controlled or prevented by the use of sprays or dusts, but others continue to puzzle the experts. Pink root is one of them.

Pink root first came into prominence during the first quarter of the century, and after more than fifty years of diligent research scientists still haven't found a way to eradicate the fungus from infected soil. But they have given us numerous hybrids and improved standard varieties of onions that are resistant to the disease.

Basal rot and neck rot are other onion diseases that fungicides have never satisfactorily controlled. With basal rot, or bottom rot, as it is sometimes called, the bulb damage may be too great for a fungicide to do any good by the time the disease is discovered.

Neck rot and pink root are responsible for heavy losses of onions every year, yet both can usually be avoided by following a few simple rules.

PINK ROOT

Pink root, caused by the fungus *Pyrenochaeta terestris*, is a major disease in many onion-growing regions, especially in the South and the West. When the disease attacks, the roots turn pink, shrivel, and die. As new roots form, they too become infected and die. This continues throughout the growing season.

The plant itself is not usually killed, but without healthy roots to nourish it, the food supply is cut so low that the resulting harvest is more like scallions or small bulbs at best.

This fungus attacks onions in all stages of growth, from the seedbed to the harvest. If the soil in the seedbed is infested, the disease will be transferred to the planting area on the roots of the transplants. Once an area is infected, the fungus seemingly lives forever, multiplying year after year.

One way to combat the problem is to start the seedbed and

The large, well-formed bulbs with healthy roots in this picture were produced on fungus-free soil, while those in the foreground grew on infested land and battled with pink root throughout the growing season, resulting in a greatly reduced yield. Courtesy Dessert Seed Co.

crop in soil in which onions have never grown before. And a rotation period of at least three years may be of value. However, neither of these plans is always reliable, because the fungus is a rather common soil inhabitant that attacks the roots of many other crops besides onions.

There is no known control for pink root. Once the soil is infested, the only solution is to plant varieties that are resistant to the disease.

Excellent progress has been made in developing such varieties. The following list includes a few of the many resistant varieties that are adapted to the South, where the disease is most prevalent: Texas Early Grano; Red and White Grano; Yellow, Red, and White Granex; Yellow, Red, and White Creole; Excel; Crystal Wax; Burgundy; Calred; Welsh onion; Beltsville bunching onion. Sweet Spanish is also somewhat resistant to the disease.

Neck rot sclerotia is one of the most serious storage rots of onions. Appearing first as a gray, powdery mass on the surface of the outer scales, the fungus spores develop into hard, black kernel-like bodies made up of finely woven fungus threads. Storage onions showing the first symptoms of this disease should be sorted out and burned to keep the infection from spreading. Courtesy Dessert Seed Co.

NECK ROT

Neck rot is one of the most serious of the fungus diseases that affect stored onions. It can be caused by any one of three *Botrytis* species, but the one commonly known as gray mold neck rot, caused by the fungus *Botrytis allii,* is the most widespread.

Onions showing the first symptoms of neck rot should be removed immediately from the storage bin, to keep them from infecting the others.

103

Although infection of the bulbs takes place in the garden, the disease does not manifest itself until after the harvest. It begins as a softening of the scale tissue and usually starts at the neck and works downward. However, it can start at a wound or bruise anywhere on the bulb.

The affected areas have a mushy, cooked appearance. They later become sunken and covered with a grayish, feltlike mat of fungus threads. If conditions are even moderately moist, spores multiply rapidly, building up on the surface as a gray, powdery mass.

Sometimes large, hard, black sclerotia—resting bodies of the fungus—appear on and between the scales. If these formations are found, they should be burned, not merely tossed out, because they can survive freezing weather and will become active again to contaminate another crop when unfavorable weather is past.

The spores of this fungus are carried on air currents. They do not infect the growing plant, but live instead on dead foliage, principally old leaves that are shed as the plant develops.

The most susceptible time for infection is just before the harvest, when the tissues of the neck area weaken and bend under the weight of the dying tops. Infection can also occur after the bulbs are dug and are curing in the rows.

Sometimes even the gardener may be instrumental in spreading the disease. In bending the tops over while they're still green—especially if the gardener uses the back of a rake—the protective membrane of the neck is broken, leaving a wound that is ideal for penetration and infection by the fungus.

Temperature and moisture conditions at the time of maturity are also contributing factors to neck rot. Cool, moist weather favors its growth while high temperatures and dry weather reduce the buildup of spores, and the disease that follows is of little consequence.

Red and yellow onions, especially the pungent varieties, are said to be more resistant than white ones. But all varieties are susceptible once penetration has taken place.

Neck rot is not a lost battle if you follow a few simple rules:

1. Allow bulbs to mature well before bending over the tops; better yet, do not bend them over. Nature will give them a nudge when it's time for them to fall.
2. Avoid bruising the bulbs, both during and after the harvest.
3. Protect the bulbs from rain and dew during the curing process.
4. Allow adequate ventilation in the storage room, with a temperature of 32° or slightly above and a relative humidity of about 65 percent.

BASAL ROT

Basal rot is caused by a soil-inhabiting fungus, *Fusarium oxysporum.* It is a widespread disease and prevalent in most onion-growing regions of the United States.

This disease is sometimes caused by a careless gardener during cultivation. If tissues are damaged, infection can enter, but it can also follow injury from other causes—pink root, maggots, wireworms, and so on.

A semiwatery decay starts at the area where the stem and roots are joined and works upward, destroying the bulb. The roots rot away, eventually disappearing entirely.

Damage resulting from the disease is well under way when symptoms appear above the ground. Leaf tips begin to yellow and die back, and, usually within a week or two, all of the foliage is dead. If infection occurs near the time of harvest, the disease can be carried into the storage bin.

As with most fungus diseases, temperature influences the growth of basal rot, both in onions in storage and in those in the garden. The cooler the temperature, the less damage this fungus will cause.

In the garden symptoms do not appear until the soil is warm. As temperatures rise, more plants become affected.

Rotation of the crop is essential in curbing this disease. When possible, the harvest should take place before soil temperatures become too high. Bulbs should be handled carefully to avoid bruising and should be inspected before storing to cull those that show signs of the disease. All discarded bulbs should be burned.

SMUT, BLACK MOLD, AND SMUDGE

The diseases known as smut, black mold, and smudge are oftentimes confused in the minds of home gardeners because of the similarity of the names and because of the way the diseases manifest their damage, particularly on onions in storage.

Smut can be eliminated from the confusion list, because plants affected with this disease seldom live long enough to produce bulbs large enough for storing. Both of the other two mar the appearance of the bulb. Smudge penetrates the bulb tissue, leaving a permanent blemish, whereas black mold usually develops on the outer skin only and can be rubbed off.

ONION SMUT

Onion smut, caused by the fungus *Urocystis cepulae,* is common in all onion-growing areas from latitude 36° northward. Because it is sensitive to heat, this fungus is of little consequence in the South.

Smut affects direct-seeded crops only and has no effect on transplants or sets, even when they are planted in smut-infested soil, providing, of course, that the plants or sets were free of the disease to begin with. The seed itself is not a carrier, but is quickly infected when planted in diseased soil.

The disease is evident at, or shortly after, germination time. It appears as a dark, slightly swollen area on the first leaf as it emerges from the ground. As later leaves appear, they too become swollen and tend to bend downward.

Most affected seedlings die within three to five weeks. Those that manage to survive produce bulbs with blisterlike lesions on and between the thick outer layers. These raised, black blisters appear at the base of the bulb as soon as it begins to form. As the bulb increases in size, the lesions may break open, releasing masses of black, sootlike spores.

Affected bulbs do not rot in storage, but they should not be

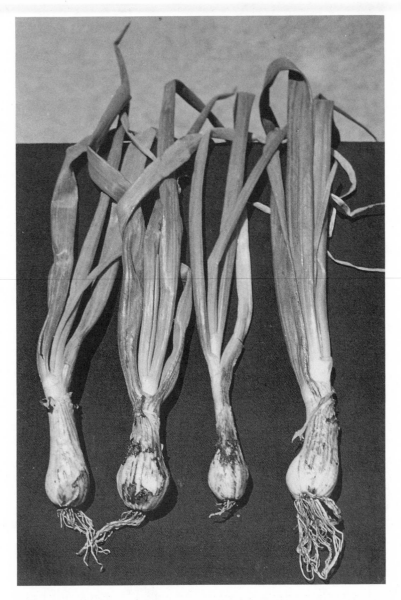

Smut lesions on onion plants are caused by soil-borne spores that infect the seedlings during a short period before emergence. Few plants survive to the stage shown in this photo. Courtesy Dessert Seed Co.

stored, as they are subject to other fungus and bacterial diseases that may attack them there.

One means of smut control is the formaldehyde-drip method, in which a stream of formaldehyde solution is applied in the furrow with the seed. This is not a permanent solution, however; it does not cure the soil, but merely disinfects it long enough for the seedling to grow past the susceptible stage.

Formaldehyde and other such fungicides are commonly used in large-scale plantings in areas where the disease is prevalent, but home gardeners usually conquer the problem by starting the onion crop with healthy sets or plants instead of seeds. Beyond the seed stage, onions have complete immunity from the disease.

All varieties of the common onion are susceptible to smut. Welsh onion, especially the nebuka type, shows the greatest resistance, although Beltsville bunching onion, a *cepa-fistulosum* hybrid, is also highly resistant.

BLACK MOLD

Black mold, caused by the fungus *Aspergillus niger*, is one of the few fungus diseases that spread more rapidly when conditions are dry.

Because it is a facultative parasite—that is, it is capable of growing on either live plants or dead—this fungus persists indefinitely as a saprophyte on organic matter in the soil. Its destructive growth continues on onion bulbs after the harvest.

In storage, black, powdery masses of spores appear as a black mold on the outer bulb scales or between them and later cause the scales to shrivel and become brittle.

Red- or brown-skinned onions are most susceptible to black mold, especially Red Creole and Australian Brown. White varieties such as Southport White Globe and White Portugal (Silverskin) are resistant.

Crop rotation is the only known method for combating black mold.

SMUDGE

Smudge, caused by the fungus *Colletotrichum circinans*, is most prevalent in the central and northeastern states. The disease does

Black mold shows as black powdery masses of spores on the outer bulb scales or between them. Later, it causes the scales to shrivel and become brittle. Losses occur both in storage, as shown here, and in the field. Courtesy Dessert Seed Co.

considerable damage to the storage crop by causing bulb shrinkage and premature sprouting, but its greatest harm lies in ruining the appearance of the bulb.

White onion varieties are susceptible, whereas those with yellow, red, or brown skins, such as Southport Red Globe, Yellow Globe Danvers, and Australian Brown, are highly resistant to the disease.

If infection does occur, it is confined mainly to the unpigmented tissues of the neck area. With white onion varieties, both the neck and the main bulb are affected.

Symptoms begin with small green and black dots, often arranged in concentric rings, on the outer scales. As the disease advances, the fungus penetrates the fleshy scales, and the spots enlarge, developing into deep, sunken areas on the bulb.

In regions where smudge is a problem, crop rotation is important, and refuse from crops produced on infested soil should be destroyed to avoid further infection.

SOFT ROT, SOUR SKIN, YELLOW DWARF, AND ASTER YELLOWS

Bacteria behave like double agents in the garden. As saprophytes feeding on dead organic material, aiding in its decomposition, and increasing the fertility of the soil, they are the gardener's friend. But when they live as parasites feeding on live plants, spreading their infectious organisms, contaminating healthy cells and tissue and causing them to decompose, they are an enemy indeed.

There are said to be at least 175 kinds of bacteria that cause disease in plants, but only 3 of these are considered to be a serious threat to onions.

Bacterial soft rot and sour, or slippery, skin are the most common. The third, caused by the bacteria *Pseudomonas alliicola*, is so rare that (as far as I know) it doesn't even have a common name. Briefly, *Pseudomonas alliicola* literally destroys the onion. Although the bulb appears perfectly sound from outside, the inner scales are water-soaked and soft, much as they would be from frost injury.

Good or bad, these single-celled microorganisms that we call bacteria are widely distributed by air, water, soil, all forms of matter, organic or otherwise, living or dead. It is possible for bacteria to enter a plant through healthy, uninjured tissue, but they more often gain entrance through wounds or lacerations. Oftentimes, insects are responsible for the wounds, and these same insects may also be carriers of the disease.

Once inside, the bacteria multiply and migrate among the cells of the plant. They may kill the cells or leave them in such an undesirable state that the plant is unfit for use.

Bacterial rots are responsible for a large share of spoilage of stored onions.

Virus diseases also cause losses, but these occur in the garden, while the plant is still growing. Most viruses that cause plant disease are transmitted by insects, principally those that have sucking mouths—aphids, leafhoppers, whiteflies, and mealybugs. Leafhoppers and aphids are responsible for two viral diseases of onions.

Pathologists list some 163 viruses that cause disease in plants, and all of these fall into two rather clearly defined groups: viruses that cause mottling or spotting of leaves; and those that cause a yellowing of the foliage, leaf curling, dwarfing, or excessive branching, but little or no mottling or spotting.

SOFT ROT

Soft rot, caused by the bacteria *Erwinia caratovora*, is one of the most destructive, as well as one of the commonest, diseases in stored onions. Organisms that cause the disease live for long periods in the soil and may infect onions even after they are removed from the garden.

The disease is not always evident at the time of storage, but may develop rapidly if storage temperatures are too warm. The rot generally begins at the neck and works down into the scales, usually those in the center of the bulb. The affected area has a glossy, water-soaked appearance and later becomes soft and mushy and has a foul odor.

Although the disease may develop rapidly, it does not spread rapidly. Usually only one or two scales are affected, and most of the bulb remains firm and healthy, making it possible to salvage this part of the bulb by trimming out the bad scales.

The bacteria causing soft rot are common in most garden soils. They develop rapidly when the weather is humid and temperatures are high. The bacteria are often carried into the onion bulb by maggots or wireworms, but they may also enter the plant through injuries from other causes: freezing, sunscald, bruises occurring during cultivation or harvesting, or from other diseases. Scullions—onions whose necks remain moist and thick instead of drying and shrinking in the usual way—are especially susceptible to the disease.

Bulbs that have been damaged by maggots or other boring insects may harbor the disease and should be culled out; healthy bulbs should be properly cured and stored in a dry, well-ventilated place.

Yellow dwarf is a virus disease that causes onion losses throughout the world. Note the variation in foliage and development of these two plants. The disease has stunted the growth of the one on the left, which should be removed and burned before it infects healthy plants, such as the one on the right. Courtesy Dessert Seed Co.

SOUR SKIN

Sour skin, or slippery skin, as it is sometimes called, is caused by the *Pseudomonas cepacia* bacterium, another threat to onions in storage.

The first symptom is a glazed or water-soaked appearance on the outer scales. These scales later disintegrate into a slimy, yellow mass with a sour, vinegarlike odor. The upper portion of the bulb shrinks and the skin slips off, leaving the center of the bulb firm and apparently healthy. This portion can be salvaged by trimming.

Affected bulbs should be removed from storage to keep the disease from spreading.

YELLOW DWARF

Yellow dwarf *(Marmor cepae)* is a worldwide onion disease. It can be transmitted from plant to plant by more than fifty species of aphids, but, strangely enough, not by thrips, mites, grasshoppers, beetles, caterpillars, or maggots. It can also be spread by mechanical means, even by the gardener handling and cutting diseased plants among healthy ones, or using knives, shears, or other garden tools without washing them after tending other plants.

The virus is not transmitted through the seed, but is often distributed by planting infected sets. If infected sets are planted, the disease will be apparent on the first leaf as it emerges. Short yellow streaks will appear at the base, and all leaves that follow will also be affected. Eventually, the whole plant becomes yellow and wrinkled, leaves droop, the stalk twists and curls, all of which give the plant a dwarfed appearance.

Welsh onion (nebuka) and Beltsville bunching onion are immune to the disease. Of the common onions, most sweet Spanish varieties, Crystal Wax (white Bermuda), Early Grano, San Joaquin, and yellow Bermuda are some varieties that are resistant to the disease.

The disease is especially severe in onions that are started from bulbs, such as shallots and potato onions. Although the Egyptian, or tree, onion does not develop symptoms of the disease, it may be a carrier of the yellow dwarf virus.

Since plants affected with this, or any, viral disease do not recover, they should be pulled up and burned to keep the infection from spreading. Prevention is the best method of control, and this is done by getting rid of the insect vectors that cause it.

Aphicides, such as rotenone or pyrethrum, both of which are nonpoisonous to humans, are available commercially. Or, homemade sprays made of tobacco stems or soapsuds are usually effective. Releasing a few handfuls of ladybugs or praying mantises into the garden will usually take care of aphids.

ASTER YELLOWS

Aster yellows, another viral disease, is carried by the six-spotted leafhopper *(Macrosteles facifrons)*. This disease also affects a number of other garden vegetables, for example, lettuce, carrots, tomatoes, celery, parsnips, salsify, and spinach, as well as many of the ornamentals growing in flower gardens.

Symptoms vary with the different types of plants, but results are pretty much the same: stunting, yellowing foliage, distorted and sterile flower heads, elongated pedicels.

Shrinking and premature sprouting occur when bulbs from infected plants are placed in storage.

Control measures for yellow dwarf and aster yellows are the same.

BLAST, LEAF AND TIP BLIGHT, DAMPING-OFF, AND SUNSCALD

While it is true that insects and fungus diseases, notably thrips, pink root, and downy mildew, are responsible for the largest share of onions losses during the growing season, a few of the so-called minor diseases also take their toll.

Although most of them are fungus-related, weather conditions prevailing at the time of infection play such an important role that oftentimes gardeners do not think of the loss as having been caused by a disease. Blast, leaf and tip blight, and damping-off are good examples.

BLAST

Blast, also known as leaf scorch or sun scorch, occurs following an abrupt change from a warm, moist growing period to one with high temperatures, low humidity, and bright sunshine. Foliage that has made succulent growth during the moist period undergoes a rapid dehydration and dies.

LEAF AND TIP BLIGHT

Leaf and tip blight, which appears during prolonged rainy periods and cool, cloudy weather, is most damaging to young thickly planted onions. Tips of the leaves become bronzed as if scorched by heat. The older, or outer, leaves, which are the ones usually affected, turn brown and die.

DAMPING-OFF

Damping-off is a disease that can wipe out a crop of onion seed-lings overnight. It may occur in the seedbed or the open garden. Three different types of damping-off are common: postemergence, preemergence, and seed rot, all of which are often blamed on the weather.

The name "damping-off" originated because of high seedling losses that occurred after plants were watered during cool, cloudy weather. The disease was thus connected with dampness.

Although it is true that the disease spreads more rapidly under such conditions, fungi in the soil cause the initial infection.

Infection spreads rapidly when seedlings are too thick, soil too moist, or air too still and humid. With postemergence damping-off, young plants with healthy-appearing leaves and roots suddenly develop a dark rotted area on the root and lower stem at or just above the soil line. This causes the seedling to topple over.

The other two types of damping-off are often mistaken for "bad" seed. If the seed is invaded with the fungus in the early stages of germination, it will not sprout, and rotting results. With preemergence damping-off, young seedlings are attacked before pushing their way through the surface of the soil, and germination failure is blamed.

The surest way to avoid damping-off is to correct the conditions that encourage it, particularly overwatering. Care must be taken while the plants are small, especially on cloudy days, and all watering should be done early in the morning so that the soil surface will have time to dry before night.

SUNSCALD

Sunscald is an environmental problem that may occur anywhere, but it is most prevalent in the hot, sunny regions of the South. It is also one that home gardeners can do something about.

Harvesting during high temperatures and very bright sunlight may result in bulbs with damaged tissue. Immature bulbs, especially of the white varieties, are most susceptible to the injury.

When sunscald occurs, the affected tissues appear bleached and are soft and slippery. As the tissues dry they become sunken and leatherlike and leave a blemish in the bulb.

Care should be taken to guard against such injuries because, aside from the blemished appearance, the affected tissues are vulnerable to soft rot, neck rot, and other diseases that can attack the bulbs in storage.

Bulb damage from sunscald is most common after the onions have been harvested, while they are still curing in the garden. However, damage may also occur before the harvest, when the maturing bulbs bulge above the ground. Preharvest sunscald can be prevented by keeping the exposed bulbs covered with loose soil or mulch until they are ready for pulling.

Injuries after harvest are usually prevented by a method called shingling. The onions are pulled with the tops intact and placed in bunches in a row so that the tops of each bunch will cover the bulbs of the previous bunch.

These simple safety measures reduce the chance of losses during the maturing period and curing operation and generally improve the flavor of the onion.

CONCLUSION

In spite of all the things that can go wrong in the onion patch, this ancient plant is still a favorite. I have members of the Allium family in my garden when there's nothing else around.

Some varieties have their resting time during the heat of our Texas summers, but they're loyal; they always come back. Old friends like common chives and garlic chives never desert me completely if I remember to keep them watered.

The more I read about onions—even in my own writing, the more I agree with the children of Israel who wandered in the wilderness, yearning for the tasty foods they left behind. Regardless of how good a cook you have in the kitchen, there are certain foods that are not complete without the flavor of onions.

Is there anything more delightful to the senses than to come in hungry from a day's work and be greeted with the onion's delicious aroma simmering in a pot of good old vegetable soup? The fragrance greets you the moment you walk in the door.

Remember the story of Jacob and Esau in Genesis 25? If Jacob had failed to put onions in the stew he cooked that day perhaps Esau wouldn't have been so eager to trade his birthright for a bowl of it.

Appendix

Alabama
Agricultural Experiment Station
Auburn University
Auburn, AL 36830

Alaska
Institute of Agricultural Sciences
University of Alaska
Fairbanks, AK 99701

Arizona
Agricultural Experiment Station
University of Arizona
Tuscon, AZ 85721

Arkansas
Agricultural Experiment Station
University of Arkansas
Fayetteville, AR 72701

California
Universitywide Admin.
Agricultural Experiment Station
University of California
Berkeley, CA 94720

Colorado
Agricultural Experiment Station
Colorado State University
Fort Collins, CO 80521

Connecticut
Agricultural Experiment Station
P.O. Box 1106
New Haven, CT 06504

Agricultural Experiment Station
University of Connecticut
Storrs, CT 06268

Delaware
Agricultural Experiment Station
University of Delaware
Newark, DE 19711

Florida
University of Florida
Institute of Food and Agricultural
    Sciences
Gainesville, FL 32601

Georgia
Agricultural Experiment Station
University of Georgia
Athens, GA 30602

Guam
Resource Development Center
University of Guam
P.O. Box EK
Agana, GU 96910

Hawaii
Agricultural Experiment Station
University of Hawaii
Honolulu, HI 96822

Idaho
Agricultural Experiment Station
University of Idaho
Moscow, ID 83843

Illinois
Agricultural Experiment Station
University of Illinois
109 Mumford Hall
Urbana, IL 61801

Indiana
Agricultural Experiment Station
Purdue University
West Lafayette, IN 47907

Iowa
Agricultural & Home Economics
  Experiment Station
Iowa State University
Ames, IA 50010

Kansas
Agricultural Experiment Station
Kansas State University
113 Waters Hall
Manhattan, KS 66506

Kentucky
Agricultural Experiment Station
University of Kentucky
Lexington, KY 40506

Louisiana
Agricultural Experiment Station
Louisiana State University and
  A&M College
Drawer E. University Station
Baton Rouge, LA 70803

Maine
Agricultural Experiment Station
University of Maine
105 Winslow Hall
Orono, ME 04473

Maryland
Agricultural Experiment Station
University of Maryland
College Park, MD 20704

Massachusetts
Agricultural Experiment Station
University of Massachusetts
Amherst, MA 01002

Michigan
Agricultural Experiment Station
Michigan State University
East Lansing, MI 48823

Minnesota
Agricultural Experiment Station
University of Minnesota
St. Paul Campus
St. Paul, MN 55101

Mississippi
Agricultural and Forestry
  Experiment Station
Mississippi State University
P.O. Drawer ES
Mississippi State, MS 39762

Missouri
Agricultural Experiment Station
University of Missouri
Columbia, MO 65201

Montana
Agricultural Experiment Station
Montana State University
Boseman, MT 59715

Nebraska
Agricultural Experiment Station
University of Nebraska
Lincoln, NE 68503

Nevada
Agricultural Experiment Station
University of Nevada
Reno, NV 89507

New Hampshire
Agricultural Experiment Station
University of New Hampshire
Durham, NH 03824

New Jersey
Agriculture Experiment Station
Rutgers University
P.O. Box 231
New Brunswick, NJ 08903

New Mexico
Agricultural Experiment Station
New Mexico State University
P.O. Box 3BF
Las Cruces, NM 88003

New York
Agricultural Experiment Station
Cornell University
Cornell Station
Ithaca, NY 14850

Agricultural Experiment Station
State Station
Geneva, NY 14456

North Carolina
Agricultural Experiment Station
North Carolina State University
Box 5847
Raleigh, NC 27601

North Dakota
Agricultural Experiment Station
North Dakota State University
State University Station
Fargo, ND 58102

Ohio
Ohio Agricultural Research and
    Development Center
Ohio State University
Columbus, OH 43210

Oklahoma
Agricultural Experiment Station
Oklahoma State University
Stillwater, OK 74074

Oregon
Agricultural Experiment Station
Oregon State University
Corvallis, OR 97331

Pennsylvania
Agricultural Experiment Station
Pennsylvania State University
229 Agricultural Admin. Bldg.
University Park, PA 16902

Puerto Rico
Agricultural Experiment Station
University of Puerto Rico
P.O. Box H
Rio Piedras, PR 00928

Rhode Island
Agricultural Experiment Station
University of Rhode Island
Kingston, RI 02881

South Carolina
Agricultural Experiment Station
Clemson University
Clemson, SC 29631

South Dakota
Agricultural Experiment Station
South Dakota State University
Brookings, SD 57006

Tennessee
Agricultural Experiment Station
University of Tennessee
P.O. Box 1071
Knoxville, TN 37901

Texas
Agricultural Experiment Station
Texas A&M University
College Station, TX 77843

Utah
Agricultural Experiment Station
Utah State University
Logan, UT 84322

Vermont
Agricultural Experiment Station
University of Vermont
Burlington, VT 05401

Virginia
Agricultural Experiment Station
Virginia Polytechnic Institute and
State University
Blacksburg, VA 24061

Virgin Islands
Agricultural Experiment Station
College of the Virgin Islands
Kingshill, St. Croix, VI 00850

Washington
Agricultural Experiment Station
Washington State University
Pullman, WA 99163

West Virginia
Agricultural Experiment Station
West Virginia University
Morgantown, WV 26506

Wisconsin
Agricultural Experiment Station
University of Wisconsin
Madison, WI 53706

Wyoming
Agricultural Experiment Station
University of Wyoming
University Station, Box 3354
Laramie, WY 82070

Bibliography

Abraham, George. *The Green Thumb Book of Fruit and Vegetable Gardening.* New Jersey: Prentice Hall, 1970.

Airola, Paavo. *The Miracle of Garlic.* Health Plus, 1978.

Angier, Bradford. *Field Guide to Edible Wild Plants.* Harrisburg, Penn.: Stackpole Books, 1974.

———. *Field Guide to Medicinal Wild Plants.* Harrisburg, Penn.: Stackpole Books, 1978.

Bailey, Liberty Hyde, and Ethel Zoe Bailey. *Hortus Second.* New York: Macmillan, 1941.

———. *Hortus Third.* Revised and expanded by the staff of the L. H. Bailey Hortorium, Cornell University. N.Y.: Macmillan, 1976.

Bailey, Ralph, ed. *Good Housekeeping Encyclopedia of Gardening.* New York: Hearst Corp, 1972.

Baker, Howard, and T. E. Hienton. "Traps Have Some Value." *Insects Yearbook.* USDA, 1952.

Baker, Howard, and O. R. Mathews. "Good Farming Helps Control Insects." *Insects Yearbook.* USDA, 1952.

Bates, Earl M. "Learning to Make the Best Use of Climate." *Insects Yearbook.* USDA, 1977.

Baumgardt, John Philip. *Bulbs for Summer Bloom.* New York: 1970.

Bennet, C. W. "Viruses, a Scourge of Mankind." *Plant Diseases Yearbook.* USDA, 1953.

Berry, James A., and F. E. Lindquist. "The Art of Drying Vegetables." *Crops in Peace and War Yearbook.* USDA, 1950–51.

Bishopp, F. C. "Insect Friends of Man." *Insects Handbook.* USDA, 1952.

Black, L. M. "How Insects Transmit Viruses." *Diseases Yearbook.* USDA, 1953.

Bliss, Beatrice. *Chinese Medicinal Herbs.* San Francisco: Georgetown Press, 1973.

Borthwick, H. A. "Day Length and Flowering." *Science in Farming Yearbook.* USDA, 1943–47.

Boswell, Victor R. "Flowering Habit and Production of Seeds." *Seeds Yearbook.* USDA, 1961.

———. "What Seeds Are and Do: An Introduction." *Seeds Yearbook.* USDA, 1961.

———, and Marlowe D. Thorne. "The Proper Use of Water in the Home Garden." *Water Yearbook.* USDA, 1955.

Bressman, E. N., and Gore Hambridge. "Fundamentals of Heredity for Breeders." *Yearbook of Agriculture.* USDA, 1937.

Bryant, M. Douglas, and Ricardo E. Gomez. "Learning to Make the Best Use of Climate: In the Southwest." *Gardening for Food and Fun Yearbook.* USDA, 1977.

Bucaro, Frank, and David Wallenchinsky. *Chico's Organic Gardening and Natural Living.* New York: Lippincott, 1972.

Burpee, W. Atlee. *Burpee's Farm Annual.* Philadelphia: W. Atlee Burpee Co., 1888.

Campbell, Mary Mason. *Kitchen Gardens.* New York: Universal, 1971.

Carleton, R. Milton. *The Small Garden Book.* New York: Universal, 1971.

———. *Vegetables for Today's Gardens.* New York: D. Van Nostrand, 1967.

Chase, A. W. *Dr. Chase's Third, Last and Complete Receipt Book.* Mich.: F. B. Dickerson & Co., 1890.

Chittenden, F. H. "Insects Injurious to the Onion Crop." *Yearbook of the United States Department of Agriculture.* USDA, 1912.

Chittenden, Fred J., ed. *The Royal Horticultural Society Dictionary of Gardening.* Cambridge: Oxford University Press, 1974.

Christenson, L. D., and Floyd F. Smith. "Insects and Plant Viruses." *Insects Yearbook.* USDA, 1952.

Claiborne, Craig. *Cooking with Herbs and Spices.* New York: Harper & Row, 1970.

Clarkson, Rosetta E. *Green Enchantment.* New York: Macmillan, 1940.

———. *Herbs: Their Culture and Uses.* New York: Macmillan, 1966.

Cook, Robert. "A Chronology of Genetics." *Yearbook of Agriculture.* USDA, 1937.

Coon, Nelson. *Dictionary of Useful Plants.* Emmaus, Penn.: Rodale Press, 1974.

———. *Using Plants for Healing.* New York: Hearthside Press Inc., 1963.

———. *Using Wayside Plants.* New York: Hearthside Press Inc., 1957.

———. *Wild Flowers of Martha's Vineyard.* Mass.: Duke's County Historical Society. 1969.

Coons, George H. "Breeding for Resistance to Disease." *Plant Diseases Yearbook*. USDA, 1953.

Corbett, L. C., et al. "Fruit and Vegetable Production." *Agriculture Yearbook*. USDA, 1925.

Crockett, James Underwood. *Crockett's Victory Garden*. Mass.: Little Brown, 1977.

Culpeper, Nicholas. *Culpeper's Compleat Herbal*. London: Foulsham & Co., n.d.

Densmore, Frances. *How Indians Used Wild Plants for Food, Medicine and Crafts*. New York: Dover, 1974.

Doeflinger, Frederic. *Complete Book of Bulb Gardening*. Harrisburg, Penn.: Stackpole Books, 1973.

Doty, Walter L. *All about Vegetables*. Calif.: Chevron, 1973.

Elbert, Virginia F., and George A. Elbert. *Fun with Growing Herbs Indoors*. New York: Crown, 1974.

Emerson, Barbara H. "Help! Help! Where You Can Find It." *Gardening for Food and Fun Yearbook*. USDA, 1977.

Everett, T. H. *The American Gardener's Book of Bulbs*. New York: Random House, 1954.

Foster, Catherine Osgood. *The Organic Gardener*. New York: Knopf, 1972.

Foster, Gertrude B. *Herbs for Every Garden*. New York: Dutton, 1966; revised edition, 1973.

Fox, Helen Morganthau. *Adventure in My Garden*. New York: Crown, 1965.

——. *Gardening for Good Eating*. New York: Collier, 1973.

——. *Gardening with Herbs for Flavor and Fragrance*. New York: Dover, 1970.

——. *The Years in My Herb Garden*. New York: Macmillan, 1953.

Fuestel, Irvin C. "The Nature and Use of Organic Amendments." *Soils and Men Yearbook*. USDA, 1938.

Gerard, John. *Of Mountaine Garlicks and of Onions*. New York: Dover, 1975.

Gibbons, Euell. *Stalking the Wild Asparagus*. New York: David McKay, 1962.

Gould, C. J. "Blights of Lilies and Tulips." *Plant Diseases Yearbook*. USDA, 1953.

Grieve, Mrs. Maud, *A Modern Herbal*. Vols. 1 and 2. New York: Dover, 1971.

Haeussler, G. J. "Losses Caused by Insects." *Insects Yearbook*. USDA, 1952.

Halprin, Ann Moyer, ed. *Unusual Vegetables*. Emmaus, Penn.: Rodale Press, 1978.

Hambridge, Gove. "Soils and Men: A Summary." *Yearbook*. USDA, 1938.

Harris, Ben Charles. *Better Health with Culinary Herbs*. Mass.: Barre, 1971.

———. *The Compleat Herbal*. New York: Larchmont, 1972.

———. *Eat the Weeds*. Mass.: Barre, 1975.

———. *Kitchen Medicines*. New York: Simon & Schuster, 1970.

———. *Kitchen Tricks*. Mass.: Barre, 1975.

Hatfield, Audrey Wynne. *How to Enjoy Your Weeds*. New York: Collier, 1971.

Hatton, Richard G. *Handbook of Plant and Floral Ornament from Early Herbals*. New York: Dover, 1960.

Hawthorn, Leslie R. "Growing Seeds for Sale." *Seeds Yearbook*. USDA, 1961.

Hedrick, U. P. *Sturdevant's Edible Plants of the World*. New York: Dover, 1972.

Horn, Anton S., and Esther H. Wilson. "Storing Fresh Fruits and Vegetables." *Gardening for Food and Fun Yearbook*. USDA, 1977.

Hottes, Alfred C. *Garden Facts and Fancies*. New York: Mead, 1949.

Hunter, Beatrice Trum. *Gardening without Poisons*. Boston, Mass.: Houghton Mifflin, 1964.

Hutchens, Alma R. *Indian Herbology in North America*. Canada: Merco, 1973.

Hutchison, John E., et al. *Onions in Texas*. Texas Agricultural Extension Service B-220. College Station: Texas A&M College System and USDA, 1953.

Hutchison, John E., Blueford G. Hancock, and Bruce A. Perry. *Reducing Vegetable Losses*. Texas Agricultural Extension Service Bulletin MP-902. College Station: Texas A&M University, 1968.

Hylton, William M., ed. *The Rodale Herb Book*. Emmaus, Penn.: Rodale Press, 1974.

Irwin, Howard S. *Roadside Flowers of Texas*. Austin: University of Texas Press, 1969.

Jacobs, Betty E. M. *All the Onions and How to Grow Them*. 1977.

Johns, Glenn F. *The Organic Way to Plant Protection*. Emmaus, Penn.: Rodale Press, 1966.

Jones, Henry A. *Hybrid Onions*. El Centro, Calif.: Dessert Seed Co., n.d.

———, and Louis K. Mann. *Onions and Their Allies.* New York: Interscience Publishers, 1963.

———. "The Story of Hybrid Onions." *USDA Yearbook,* 1943–1947.

Kamm, Minnie Watson. *Old-Time Herbs for Northern Gardens.* New York: Dover, 1971.

King, Eleanor Anthony. *Bible Plants for American Gardens.* New York: Dover, 1975.

Kolaga, Walter A. *All about Rock Gardens and Plants.* New York: Doubleday, 1966.

Kraft, Ken, and Pat Kraft. *The Best of American Gardening.* New York: Walker, 1975.

Krochmal, Arnold, and Connie Krochmal. *A Guide to Medicinal Plants.* New York: Quadrangle, 1975.

Kyle, Jack H., and Cecil Regier. *Onion Variety Trials on the Northern High Plains.* Progress Report 2538, Texas Agricultural Extension Service. College Station: Texas A&M University, 1970.

Larsen, John, Tom Longbrake, and Sam Cotner. *Keys to Profitable Onion Production in Texas.* MP 971, Texas Agricultural Extension Service. College Station: Texas A&M University, 1970.

Larsen, John E. *Planning Your Vegetable Garden.* Fact Sheet L-911. Texas Agricultural Extension Service. College Station: Texas A&M University, 1970.

Leach, J. G. "Bacteria, Fungi and Insects." *Insects Yearbook.* USDA, 1953.

———. "Insects, Bacteria and Insects." *Insects Yearbook.* USDA, 1952.

Leeper, Paul, H. T. Blackhurst, and Clyde C. Singletary. *Growing Garlic in Texas.* Texas Agricultural Extension Service L-454. College Station: Texas A&M University, 1961.

Leighty, Clyde E. "Crop Rotation." *Soils and Men Yearbook.* USDA, 1938.

Lewis, R. D., and K. S. Quisenberry. "Policies on the Release of Seeds." *Seeds Yearbook.* USDA, 1961.

Longbrake, Tom. *Easy Gardening . . . Onions.* Texas Agricultural Extension Service L-1580. College Station: Texas A&M University, 1979.

Lust, John. *The Herb Book.* New York: Bantam Books, 1974.

McMurtrey, J. E., Jr. "Environmental, Nonparasitic Dangers." *Plant Diseases Yearbook.* USDA, 1953.

Medsger, Oliver Perry. *Edible Wild Plants.* New York: Collier, 1976.

Meyer, Clarence. *Fifty Years of the Herbalist Almanac.* Glenwood, Ill.: Meyerbooks, 1977.

Miles, Bebe. *The Wonderful World of Bulbs.* New York: Van Nostrand, 1963.

Miller, Paul R. "The Effect of Weather on Diseases." *Plant Diseases Yearbook.* USDA, 1953.

Miloradivich, Milo. *The Art of Cooking with Herbs and Spices.* Garden City, N.Y.: Doubleday, 1950.

Moore, Harold E. *The Cultivated Alliums.* Vols. I and II. Ithaca, N.Y.: Cornell University Press, 1954. Vols. III and IV, 1955.

Morgan, M. F., J. H. Gourley, and J. K. Albeiter. "The Soil Requirements of Economic Plants." *Soils and Men Yearbook.* USDA, 1938.

Morton, J. Sterling, et al. "Methods of Controlling Injurious Insects." *Yearbook of the Department of Agriculture.* USDA, 1896.

Mueller, Charles H. *Bulbs for Beauty.* New York: Barrows, 1947.

Muesebeck, C. F. W. "What Kind of Insect Is It?" *Insects Yearbook.* USDA, 1952.

Newton, Weldon H., et al. *Insects Attacking Vegetable Crops.* Texas Agricultural Extension Service B-1019. College Station: Texas A&M University, 1914.

Niering, W. A., and N. C. Olmstead. *The Audubon Society Field Guide to North American Wild Flowers Eastern Region.* New York: Knopf, 1979.

Nikiforoff, Constanin C. "Soil Organic Matter and Soil Humus." *Soils and Men Yearbook.* USDA, 1938.

Null, Gary, and Steve Null. *Herbs for the Seventies.* New York: Robert Speller and Sons, 1972.

Ogden, Samuel R. *Step-by-Step Organic Gardening.* Emmaus, Penn.: Rodale Press, 1971.

Organic Gardening and Farming Editors. *Best Ideas for Organic Gardening.* Emmaus, Penn.: Rodale Press, 1969.

———. *The Calendar of Organic Gardening.* Emmaus, Penn.: Rodale Press, 1975.

Parkinson, John. *A Garden of Pleasant Flowers:* Paradisi *in* Sole Paradisus Terrestris. New York: Dover, 1976.

Pellegrini, Angelo M. *The Food Lover's Garden.* New York: Knopf, 1970.

Pesman, M. Walter. *Meet the Natives.* Colorado: Smith-Brooks Printing Co. 1948.

Philbrick, Helen, and Richard Gregg. *Companion Plants and How to Use Them.* Conn: Devin-Adair, 1970.

Philbrick, John, and Helen Philbrick. *The Bug Book: Harmless Insect Controls.* Mass.: Philbrick, 1963.

Pieters, A. J., and Roland McKee. "The Use of Cover and Green-Manure Crops." *Soils and Men Yearbook.* USDA, 1938.

Ramsey, G. B. "Market Diseases Caused by Fungi." *Plant Diseases Yearbook.* USDA, 1953.
———— "Mechanical and Chemical Injuries." *Plant Diseases Yearbook.* USDA, 1953.
Raymond, Dick. *Down-to-Earth Vegetable Gardening.* Charlotte, Vt.: Gardenway, 1975.
————, and Jan Raymond. *The Gardens for All Book of Onions.* Vt.: John O. Davies, 1978.
Reed, L. B., and S. P. Doolittle. *Insects and Diseases of Vegetables in the Home Garden.* Home and Garden Bulletin No. 46. USDA, 1961.
————. *Insects and Diseases of Vegetables in the Home Garden.* Home and Garden Bulletin No. 380. USDA, 1975.
Remington, Joseph, et al. *The Dispensatory of the United States of America.* 20th ed. Philadelphia: Lippincott, 1918.
Riker, A. J., and A. C. Hildebrandt. "Bacteria—Small and Mighty." *Plant Diseases Yearbook.* USDA, 1953.
Riotte, Louise. *Companion Planting for Successful Gardening.* Charlotte, Vt.: Gardenway Publishing, 1975.
————. *Planetary Planting.* New York: Simon & Schuster, 1975.
Rodale, J. I., and staff. *Encyclopedia of Organic Gardening.* Emmaus, Penn.: Rodale Press, 1961.
————. *How to Grow Vegetables and Fruits by the Organic Method.* Emmaus, Penn.: Rodale Press, 1961.
Rodale, Robert. *The Basic Book of Organic Gardening.* New York: Ballantine Books, 1971.
Rosengarten, Frederic, Jr. *The Book of Spices.* New York: Pyramid, 1973.
Schneider, L. I., and Robert Stone. *Old Fashioned Remedies That Work Best.* New York: Parker, 1971.
Scully, Virginia. *A Treasury of American Indian Herbs: Their Lore and Their Use for Food, Drugs, and Medicine.* New York: Crown, 1970.
Seymour, John. *The Self-sufficient Gardener.* New York: Doubleday, 1979.
Shih-Chen, Li. *Chinese Medicinal Herbs.* California: Georgetown Press. 1973. First published in China 1578. Translated and researched by F. Porter Smith, M. D., and G. A. Stuart, M.D. Edited by Beatrice Bliss.
Simmonite, W. J., and Nicholas Culpeper. *The Simmonite-Culpeper Herbal Remedies.* New York: Award Books, 1957.
Smith, Perry M. "Learning to Make the Best Use of Climate: In the Southeast." *Gardening for Food and Fun Yearbook.* USDA, 1977.

Smith, Wilson, Jr., and B. A. Friedman. "The Diseases Bacteria Cause in the Home Garden." *Plant Diseases Yearbook.* USDA, 1953.

Spellenberg, Richard. *The Audubon Society Field Guide to North American Wildflowers, Western Region.* New York: Knopf, 1979.

Spencer, Edwin Rollin. *All about Weeds.* New York: Dover. 1957.

Sperry, O. E., et al. *Texas Plants Poisonous to Livestock.* Texas Agricultural Service Bulletin No. 1028. College Station: Texas A&M University, n.d.

Steere, William C., et al. *Wildflowers of the United States.* Vol. 3. New York: Knopf, 1979.

Stevens, Russel B. "The Fungi Are Living Organisms." *Plant Diseases Yearbook.* USDA, 1953.

Stevenson, Frederick J., and Henry A. Jones. "Some Sources of Resistance in Crop Plants." *Plant Diseases Yearbook.* USDA, 1953.

Stirm, Walter L. "Learning to Make the Best Use of Climate in the Northeast." *Gardening for Food and Fun Yearbook.* USDA, 1977.

Stout, Ruth, and Richard Clemence. *Ruth Stout's No-Work Gardening Book.* Emmaus, Penn.: Rodale Press, 1960, 1971.

Tampion, John. *Dangerous Plants.* New York: Universe Books, 1977.

Tatum, Billy Joe. *Billy Joe Tatum's Wild Foods Cookbook and Field Guide.* New York: Workman, 1976.

Taylor, Albert L. "The Tiny but Destructive Nematodes." *Plant Diseases Yearbook.* USDA, 1953.

Taylor, Kathryn S., and Stephen F. Hamblin. *Handbook of Wild Flower Cultivation.* New York: Collier, 1963.

Taylor, Norman. *Taylor's Encyclopedia of Gardening.* Boston: Houghton-Mifflin, 1960.

Taylor, Norman. *Taylor's Garden Guide.* New Jersey: Van Nostrand, 1957.

Thomas, H. Rex, and W. J. Zaumeyer. "Developing Healthier Vegetables." *Plant Diseases Yearbook.* USDA, 1953.

Thrower, Percy. *Fresh Vegetables and Herbs from Your Garden.* New York: Crescent Books, 1974.

Thurber, Nancy, and Gretchen Mead. *Keeping the Harvest.* Charlotte, Vt.: Gardenway, 1976.

Van Bruggen, Theodore. *Wild Flowers of the Northern Plains and Black Hills.* S.D.: Badlands Natural History Association in cooperation with the National U.S. Dept. of Interior, 1971.

Vandemark, J. S. "Onions Are Finicky as to Growing, Curing: And Garlic May Not Be a Joy Either." *Gardening for Food and Fun Yearbook.* USDA, 1977.

Waite, M. B., et al. "Diseases and Pests of Fruits and Vegetables." *Agriculture Yearbook.* USDA, 1925.

Walker, J. C. "Hazards to Onions in Many Areas." *Plant Diseases Yearbook.* USDA, 1953.

———. "Onion Curing to Prevent Decay." *The Year in Agriculture Yearbook.* USDA, 1925.

Watt, Berniece K., and A. L. Merrill. *Composition of Foods.* Agriculture Handbook No. 8. USDA, 1950.

Weiner, Michael A. *Earth Medicines—Earth Foods.* New York: Macmillan, 1972.

Wescott, Cynthia. *The Gardener's Bug Book.* New York: Doubleday, 1964.

Weslager, C. A. *Magic Medicines of the Indians.* N.J.: Middle Atlantic Press, 1973.

Wester, Robert E. *Growing Vegetables in the Home Garden.* New York: Dover, 1975.

———. *Surburban and Farm Vegetable Gardens.* Home and Garden Bulletin No. 9. USDA, 1967.

Wigginton, Eliot. *The Foxfire Book.* Garden City: Doubleday, 1972.

———. *Foxfire 2.* Garden City: Anchor Press–Doubleday, 1973.

———. *Foxfire 3.* Garden City: Anchor Press–Doubleday, 1975.

Williams, Thomas A. *The Old Dirt Dobber's Garden.* New York: Robert M. McBride & Co., 1944.

Wingard, S. A. "The Nature of Resistance to Disease." *Plant Diseases Yearbook.* USDA, 1953.

Wren, R. W. *Potter's Cyclopedia of Medicinal Herbs and Preparations.* New York: Harper & Row, 1972.

Wright, T. R. "Physiological Disorders." *Plant Diseases Yearbook.* USDA, 1953.

Wyman, Donald. *The Saturday Morning Gardener.* New York: Macmillan. 1972.

———. *Wyman's Gardening Encyclopedia.* New York: Macmillan. 1971.

Yepson, Roger B., Jr. *Organic Plant Protection.* Emmaus, Penn.: Rodale Press, 1976.

Index